MW01520235

Marie-Louise von Franz, Honorary Patron

Studies in Jungian Psychology
by Jungian Analysts

Daryl Sharp, General Editor

ANOTHER PIECE
OF MY HEART

with
Badger McGee
(Sett in His Eros Ways)

The Badger Trilogy, Book 2

DARYL SHARP

For Bo Peep, Rebecca/Sophia, EL Jay, and Ships At Sea.

Thanks to Library of America for the Emerson passages, Princeton University Press for quotes from Jung's *Collected Works*, and Random House for passages from Jung's *Memories, Dreams, Reflections.*

Library and Archives Canada Cataloging in Publication

Sharp, Daryl, 1936-, author
Another piece of my heart : with Badger McGee (sett in his eros ways) :
the Badger trilogy, book 2 / Daryl Sharp.

(Studies in Jungian psychology by Jungian analysts ; 141)
Includes bibliographical references and index.
ISBN 978-1-894574-43-3 (pbk.)

1. Love-—Psychological aspects. 2. Jungian psychology. I. Title. II. Title: Badger trilogy. Book 2. III. Series: Studies in Jungian psychology by Jungian analysts ; 141

BF175.5.L68S52 2014   152.4'1   C2014-900073-1

Copyright © 2014 by Daryl Sharp.
All rights reserved.

INNER CITY BOOKS
Box 1271, Station Q, Toronto, ON M4T 2P4, Canada.
Telephone 416) 927-0355. NO FAX.
Toll.free in Canada and U.S.: 1-888-927-0355
www.innercitybooks.net / **booksales@innercitybooks.net**

Honorary Patron: Marie-Louise von Franz.
Publisher and General Editor: Daryl Sharp.
Senior Editor: Victoria B. Cowan.
Office Manager: Scott Milligen.
Editorial Assistance: Sharpconnections.com, J. Morgan.

INNER CITY BOOKS was founded in 1980 to promote the understanding and practical application of the work of C. G. Jung.

Cover images: Photo of the author, and rendering of the publishing house, Inner City Books.

Printed and bound in Canada by Thistle Printing Limited.

CONTENTS

See final pages for other Inner City titles and how to order

"Because the world is round, it turns me on."
—The Beatles.

"There is a crack in everything. That's how the light gets in."
—Leonard Cohen.

"Hey Babe, just follow the drums and bass and you'll be fine."
—Lena Horne to Sarah Vaughan.

"Do not go where the path may lead, go instead where there is no path and leave a trail."
—Ralph Waldo Emerson.

"Thursday exists so that Wednesday and Friday don't collide."
—Peter O'Toole, in the film *Dean Spanley*.

"There will always be the bulk of people out there who are straight."
— Janis Joplin.

"You know you got it when it makes you feel good."
—Janis again.

"Freedom is just another word for nothin' left to lose."
—Kris Kristofferson.

"There is time so that everything doesn't happen all at once."
—Albert Einstein.

"Jazz makes you cooler."—Tim Tamashiro, on Tonic (CBC).

"The trouble with a complex is that it has no imagination."
—James Hollis.

"We live our fantasies thanks to complexes and projection."
—Daryl Sharp.

PREFACE

There is no good reason for me to be writing this book except that I want to. Blame it on my writing complex, that's true enough. Or call it a whimsical adventure in nonsense, interspersed with the pure quill. That's true too.

I think that in this book I will eschew rock 'n' roll, my favorite genre of music, but I will make free with jazzy love songs that embody Eros.

Here is a taste of the tone or mood I have in mind:

> Skylark
> Have you anything to say to me
> Won't you tell me where my love can be
> Is there a meadow in the mist
> Where someone's waiting to be kissed
>
> Skylark
> Have you seen a valley green with spring
> Where my heart can go a-journeying
> Over the shadows and the rain
> To a blossom covered lane
>
> And in your lonely flight
> Haven't you heard the music of the night
> Wonderful music, faint as a will o' the wisp
> Crazy as a loon
> Sad as a gypsy serenading the moon
>
> Skylark
> I don't know if you can find these things
> But my heart is riding on your wings
> So if you see them anywhere
> Won't you lead me there?[1]

---

[1] Linda Ronstadt, "Skylark," lyrics and music by Johnny Mercer and Hoaggy Carmichael; Ascap.

Introduction
Badger Cull in England?

England is about to cull 5,000 badgers, asserting that they spread bovine TB. Some scientists are against it. Badger lovers are bereft.

Despite petitions, threats from animal rights activists, and Parliamentary debate, a controversial badger cull is under way in England, the BBC reports.

A badger, for those not acquainted with the species, is a mammal about three feet long with gray fur, a mouthful of sharp teeth, and a black-and-white face striped like a zebra crossing. *Meles meles*, the European badger, is indigenous to the United Kingdom, lives in an underground labyrinth of tunnels called a sett, and feeds on worms and grubs. There are about 300,000 badgers in England. They have been around long enough to have survived two ice ages, but thanks to a Conservative-dominated coalition government plan, some 5,000 will not survive a culling policy that aims to reduce the spread of tuberculosis (known to be carried by badgers) in cattle.

In 1971, a dead badger was discovered in a barn in Gloucester, autopsied, and found to be infected with TB. The concern—that badgers transmit the bacterium to cows, thereby putting a farm at risk of being shut down until the infection has cleared—has enmeshed scientists, politicians, government bureaucrats, and farmers ever since.

Opposition Gathers Steam

Last year, the Department for Environment, Food and Rural Affairs (DEFRA) announced its intention to test the "safety, humaneness, and efficacy" of culling by targeting 5,000 badgers in Gloucestershire and Somerset—two infection hot spots.

As the proposed cull drew closer, the controversy widened to include celebrities like Queen guitarist Brian May, who led a protest march in London in June and recorded a song called "Badger Swagger"; the rock star Meatloaf; and actress Dame Judi Dench, who posted a video on YouTube calling for a stop to culling.

An anti-culling petition drew hundreds of thousands of signers, and there's an online threat of a voodoo curse on Environmental Secretary Owen Patterson, a hard-line advocate of the cull. Others have weighed in with tweets, blogs, and letters to the editors of British newspapers. "Cull the politicians instead," one reader wrote in the *Daily Mail*. On the other side, a farmer's wife pointed out that "we wouldn't be having any of this nonsense if this was about culling rats."

Costly Issue

According to DEFRA, bovine TB cost taxpayers £100 million last year. Over the next decade costs are estimated to rise to £1 billion. In the late 1990s, the government appointed an independent commission to study the problem. Ten years and £50 million later, the report, "Bovine TB: The Scientific Evidence," concluded that the overall benefits of proactive culling were modest, and that "given its high costs and low benefits we conclude that badger culling is unlikely to contribute usefully to the control of cattle TB."

A DEFRA spokesperson disputes that, however, and says that since the report was published, further research has shown that the benefits of reducing TB remain for many years after culling has stopped. According to a DEFRA statement, "No other country has successfully tackled bovine TB without addressing infection in both wildlife and cattle."

Bovine TB is rarely transmitted to humans—the number of cases in the UK is very small, and pasteurization kills the bacteria in milk. It is possible, says Nigel Gibbons, DEFRA's chief veterinarian, for people who work or live closely with infected animals to contract TB by inhaling the bacteria or coming into contact with the animals' secretions.

The economic impact on farmers whose cows test positive, however, can be profound. A farmer whose operation is shut down by infection can be out of business until the infection clears, which could take months; the cows are, in effect, quarantined. TB vaccination for cattle and badgers has its own set of complications. Current testing is not sophisticated enough to distinguish between cows vaccinated for TB and those infected by it. The effectiveness of the injected badger vaccination, depending on whose figure you take, is between 65 and 73 percent. Studies are going forward to develop a better oral vaccine for badgers, as well as a more sophisticated test for bovine TB in cows.

The controversy is full of biological complexities, colored by politics, and awash in contentious statements. "The policy appears to be little more than a sop to [the] farming sector," the executive director of the Humane Society International/UK wrote in a piece on the website Badgergate. "The only way we can do this [control bovine TB] is to cull," the head of the British Veterinary Association told the *Telegraph*.

Look Out, Mr. Badger

Plans are to use professional marksmen with rifles and shotguns over a six-week period. Animal rights activists have threatened to disrupt culling activity, though Avon and Somerset Chief Constable Nick Gargan told the BBC his force has been prepared.

"It will end up in a mess," predicts Chris Cheeseman, a former scientific adviser to the government who has spent 35 years studying badgers. "It's not supported by science. It will not solve the problem. It is not cost-effective. And it will probably make it worse."

The debate has some quintessentially British aspects to it. "To some extent, it's a rerun of the fox-hunting debate, a split between town and country," explained cultural anthropologist Sean Carey, a research fellow at the University of Roehampton's Department of Social Science. "The townie has a romanticized version of the badger, which has a privileged place in English literature. Mr. Badger in *The Wind in the Willows* is an outsider but has heroic qualities. The country farmer, on the other hand, prides himself on realism. It's a case of 'let's get rid of the sentiment and get practical.'

Woe Poor Badgers

Curious as to what this might do to the food web. I do not believe it should be done simply because of pressure from cow farms. I'm sure there are other ways for farmers to limit cow interaction with badgers, instead of we humans playing god once more.

All I can say is just because we can kill does not mean we have to. I live in Tasmania, and when wallaby populations grow they cull them as well. Badgers have been on this planet a lot longer than us and have more right being here than us; stupid politics to keep farmers happy, makes me mad, killing any wild animal should be a crime.

Gavin Bletchley writes:

Living in Alberta, Canada, I often hear farmers jabbering about their hunts... and it seems that once they start killing, they can't stop themselves. Once they have a gun in their hands, they turn crazy and shoot everything that moves. They start with Prairie dogs and Squirrels, then move on to Skunks, Coyotes, Porcupine.... and finish with Woodpeckers, Magpies, Songbirds.... and the list goes on and on. If UK starts doing that.... what happens in the Prairies of North America will more than likely happen there.

Here, I saw the government give bounties for Wolf and Coyote pelts because there were "too many". They didn't give any limit of kills; the rule was bring in as many as you can so their numbers decrease. They didn't worry about loss of genetic diversity, or about the consequences on the prairie population due to having only a few Wolves and Coyotes left. They only worried about their cash, and what cost the least, and that's the problem of our world today. Leaders only think of cash, money, and their own benefits, regardless of the consequences in the future. Leaders only go with what's easy and what pays now, but very few do what's best and what's right.

What about the "person" who has just had enough of human beings killing everything in their path?

One must surely wonder that this proposal has actually started. It's taken them long enough, endless tea breaks no doubt all courtesy of the British taxpayer. As the report says, Bovine TB is rarely transmitted to humans, plus there is a pasteurization process. I thought my government were a pack of weirdos. I obviously thought right.

Just another example of the stupid British ideal of removing the problem by destroying it. . . Its complete nonsense and ultimately just another smokescreen to distract the confused public from their other "bent" affairs!

It has come to my attention that BTB is possibly transferred to domestic pets; should we cull them too? say good bye to poor old puss or fido? I think not!

This has nothing to do with being humane or the beef industry, which I might add, worldwide is responsible for massive climate change! It's all political. We must put a stop to this right now: petition, protest, get in the way and be active!

I do not think any farmer worth his salt wants to see badgers being culled. The science states the culling of badgers will not stop BTB. Would it not be better to spend the money on a treatment for TB in badgers rather than to pay people to shoot them?

Round up 1000 of the badgers before the Tories can kill them all, GMO them with rottweiller anger, dump 'em in Parliament and lock the doors. That would constitute the greatest culling of the 21st century.

Mr Carey needs to understand that this is not about romance, it is about science and protection of British wildlife.

When randomised badger culling trials took place to form the Independent Scientific Groups final report, only one in seven badgers were found to be infected by BTB. The ISG final report said that badger culling is unlikely to contribute usefully to the control of BTB in Britain and recommend that TB control efforts focus on measures other than badger culling. These trials cost the country the best part of £50 million. Why has this been ignored?

I feel sorry for the farmers as they are the ones who will feel the true backlash of this. People will stop supporting them. Look at any online poll to do with badger culling and it is always a huge majority against it. Farmers need to wake up, they need to tell DEFRA and the NFU this is NOT the way to go. This is their livelihoods—vaccinate to eradicate.

"The culling of badgers is not the answer to the control of BTB in cattle," says Lord John Krebs, the country's most knowledgeable scientist.[2]

---

[2] From National Geographic Society, Washington, DC, August, 2013.

1
BADGER MCGEE
Sett in My Eros Ways

Oh Britannia, Britannia cull me not. I am but a foolish, hapless, harmless underground creature who keeps the soil enlivened and tourists happy.

> I'm comin' in outa the dark.
> I got soul and I got heart.
> but it ain't easy comin' outa the dark.

After culling, I am afraid of fire, falling down the stairs, home invasion, ill-tempered women, climate change and impotence. Just wanted to get that out of the way. I am an elderly badger, after all, and I have almost-human feelings.

My fur is nearly all gone and my teeth are slowly falling out. Have patience, eventually I'll cull myself.

Honey Badger wine label

Lured by the Honeyguide bird to the tempting dangers of the beehive, Africa's Honey Badger attacks with little regard for the stinging consequences, reaping the sweet reward of teamwork.

This undeterred attitude and unlikely partnership inspired the identity of this boldly luscious red that panders to those who prefer their wine rich, ripe and sumptuously fruity. Smooth, succulent and simply delicious socially or with red meat on the BBQ, mature yellow cheese or berry-inspired desserts.[3]

****

In Eros, Naturally, the first book of this trilogy, I was hijacked by my patron Daemon. Perhaps foolishly, I let him roam without a leash. It wasn't all bad, but really, to say the truth, he is a civilized, aculturated, sentient beast and not particularly wise to our wilderness ways. Never-

---

[3] W.O. Western Cape.

theless, I hold no grudge. I will give his voice an appropriate place in this book, with no reprisals. I even forgive his propensity to write, for I have a similar complex.

I concede that Daemon and his shadowy associate Razr are the more lascivious (of we three), but I hesitate to accept that along with such an inclination goes a greater appreciation of Eros, sensuality and what it may lead to when expressed, on dance floor, in bedroom or back alley. I do not mean to boast here, nor to embarrass my dear partner Bo Peep, but before she and I were betrothed, I cut a rake-hell swath throughout Europe and the British Empire. Meanwhile, Bo Peep, though virginal from kneecap to fettle, did shyly enjoy the attention of handsome young courtiers. I loved her on sight with primordial zeal.

Now, don't misunderstand me. I was no 007, but I was in a position to pocket some small fortunes Bond left behind in pursuit of saving fair ladies. Hence my current comfortable circumstances and the freedom to pursue legitimate business concerns, such as a thriving bagel shop with wood oven in downtown Toronto and this barely-viable publishing enterprise (in league with Daemon) devoted to the work of Jungian analysts. But on the whole, I am a badger of leisure, and I usually sleep till noon.

It is not my way to lay blame or seek out right or wrong. I will merely be authentic, state the facts as I know them and let readers draw their own conclusions, if they have a mind for it.

Well, let us live our nonsense and may Gnu take the hindmost.

****

Besides the revolutionary BOOK (Bio-Optic Organized Knowledge device), heralded in EROS, NATURALLY as a new-age vehicle for reading, one must not forget the pre-digital-age implement known as PEN (Perfect Eros Naturally), and its close associate PENCIL (Pursuing Eros Naturally Causes Illicit Love Affairs).[4]

****

---

[4] Thanks to friend and fellow analyst Rebecca/Sophia.

But what of real life?—

It begins to tell,
Round midnight, midnight.
I do pretty well, till after sundown,
Suppertime I'm feelin' sad;
But it really gets bad,
Round midnight.

Memories always start round midnight
Haven't got the heart to stand those memories,
When my heart is still with you,
And ol' midnight knows it, too.
When a quarrel we had needs mending,
Does it mean that our love is ending.

Darlin' I need you, lately I find
You're out of my heart,
And I'm out of my mind.
Let our hearts take wings
Round midnight, midnight

Let the angels sing,
For your returning.
Till our love is safe and sound.
And old midnight comes around.
Feelin' sad,
Really gets bad
Round, round, round, midnight.[5]

I chose this rather sad song because it is a masterpiece in jazz that is widely considered to be the pinnacle of the genre.

Pardon me, but I do tend to become maudlin and sentimental in the early a.m. So do most badgers. As I said, I bin almost human, if it weren't for my furry feet and adorable snout. And I can touch-type sixty words a minute. Bet you didn't expect that.

Now I want to pair "Round Midnight" with another melancholy song,

---

[5] Music by Thelonious Monk, lyrics by Cootie Williams; Ascap.

this one decidedly a jazz standard that opens a pit of angst:

> What's new?
> How is the world treating you?
> You haven't changed a bit
> Lovely as ever, I must admit
>
> What's new?
> How did that romance come through?
> We haven't met since then
> Gee, but it's nice to see you again
>
> What's new?
> Probably I'm boring you
> But seeing you is grand
> And you were sweet to offer your hand
>
> I understand. Adieu!
> Pardon my asking what's new
> Of course you couldn't know
> I haven't changed, I still love you so.[6]

****

Meanwhile, I keep thinking of the Harrods' rooftop dolly who took a fancy to me and then enticed me onto her futon in a flat on Tottenham Court Road in London UK. She was really sweet and asked nothing but that I hold her close and massage her buxom body. So why can't I remember her name or anything else about her? I wasn't of a mind to take notes at that time, so I have no record.

I am ashamed that in my unconscious youth I treated a woman so fecklessly. Well, I had no notion of Eros then. I was just twenty-two and had maths and physics on the brain. So sue me, and almost everyone else who's lived since the Renaissance and forgotten the Epicurean tradition celebrating the pursuit of pleasure (silenced largely due to the Inquisition of the Catholic Church and Christianity's promotion of pain and suffering as the path to Heaven).

Okay, so let's put it all up front—shadow. I think this whole book

---

[6] Frank Sinatra ,"What's New?" written by Burke/Haggart; Ascap.

should be about shadow, practical and theoretical, or else it is better not written at all. But the question is, can it be true too? I mean, who is writing, me, Daemon, or my/his shadow? Well, we'll get to that in due course. For the nonce, savor these lyrics:

> Well, you're a sweetheart
> If there ever was one
> If there ever was one
> Baby, it's you
>
> Don't you know life without you
> Was an incomplete dream
> You are every sweet dream
> Come true
>
> My search was such a blind one
> And I was all at sea
> I never thought I'd find one
> Quite so perfect for me
>
> Yes, you're a sweetheart
> If there ever was one
> If there ever was one
> Baby, it's you
>
> Oh, you're a sweetheart
> If there ever was one
> If there ever was one
> It's you
>
> Oh, oh, baby, it's you
> Yeah, yeah, yeah, yeah, yeah
> Baby, it's you.[7]

****

Now I am feeling melancholy too, and struck by an old memory:

---

[7] Frank Sinatra, "You're a Sweetheart," music and lyrics by Jimmy McHugh and Harold Adamson; Ascap.

Ode to Mary Lynn

Do you sigh,
As do I,
For our lost love?
Do you cry,
As do I,
For our love lost?

Do you think we might have made it
If I hadn't fooled around
With that little popsie
In the Hebrides?
She meant nothing to me
But a roll in the Hey, Hey
Hydee-Ho.
Hope you know
You are my all.

Speaking of shadow, the collective is absolutely toxic, not only for bikes and cars on city roads and busy highways, but psychologically for everyone. The collective is a morass of conformity and power-driven politics; in short, it is toxic and a rat's ass. Individuality is generally not welcomed by the collective, let alone prized, though paradoxically the whimsical work of artists is often lauded.

I love Bo Peep, but lookee here, that's a cute dolly in the next booth. I imagine:

"Hey there, can I buy you a drink?"

"Don't mind if you do," she smiles.

And now, what might that lead to? I half-hoped she'd say she was waiting for someone, or just tell me to get lost. Should I pursue this possible erotic adventure? I wondered. Infidelity does not come naturally to me, but she is so pretty....

That is the task of our age, to live with ambiguity and paradox.

****

Now here is Eros, naturally—Carole King singing:

When you're down and troubled
And you need some loving care
And nothing, nothing is going right
Close your eyes and think of me
And soon I will be there
To brighten up even your darkest night

You just call out my name
And you know wherever I am
I'll come running to see you again
Winter, spring, summer or fall
All you have to do is call
And I'll be there
You've got a friend

If the sky above you
Grows dark and full of clouds
And that old north wind begins to blow
Keep your head together
And call my name out loud
Soon you'll hear me knocking at your door

You just call out my name
And you know wherever I am
I'll come running to see you again
Winter, spring, summer or fall
All you have to do is call
And I'll be there
Ain't it good to know that you've got a friend

When people can be so cold
They'll hurt you and desert you
And take your soul if you let them

Oh, but don't you let them
You just call out my name
And you know wherever I am
I'll come running to see you again
Winter, spring, summer or fall

All you have to do is call
And I'll be there
You've got a friend.[8]

****

5 a.m., and I am still pushing the envelope in trying to say what I mean, and meaning what I say. It's not so easy, this writing business. Not my fault, just the messenger.

****

Here is Ralph Waldo Emerson on friendship:

> The end of friendship is a commerce the most strict and homely that can be joined, more strict than any of which we have experience. It is for aid and comfort through all the relations of life and death. It is fit for serene days, and graceful gifts, and country rambles, but also for rough roads and hard fare, shipwreck, poverty, and persecution. It keeps company with the sallies of the wit and the trances of religion. We are to dignify to each other the daily needs and offices of man's life, and embellish it by courage wisdom, and unity. It should never fall into something usual and settled, but should be alert and inventive, and add rhyme and reason to what was drudgery.[9]

In Badgerland we have a saying: "Don't do today what you can put off until tomorrow." Well, you can imagine what never gets done, and nobody notices… Well, when nothing's going right, go left.

Bo Peep left me last week to visit her husband in Buffalo. Hitchhiking even! No real surprise there, but I am left lonesome and yearning. So much for my proclivity for falling in love with attached lady badgers. I don't know what to do about this except to find someone new to love— unattached. But this is not easily done at my age, especially since I am loath to leave my sett to go out looking. I mean, pursuing dates with other lonely badgers takes a lot of energy. I've done it a few times and in the event I've found such encounters unrewarding.

---

[8] "You got a friend";Ascap.
[9] *Essays, First and Second Series,* pp. 118f.

So, I give up (well, for now). I will live alone and write my books, and let Dante take the hindmost. (Pardon this literary reference; it just slipped out because, as agnostic as I may be, I fear Purgatory and the Inferno as much as home invasion.)

****

Thursday and Friday

My dear Badgerette, back from Buffalo, was in a snit and I did not know why. Something I said or did, something she ate? I didn't have a clue. Relationship is an enigma wrapped in a conundrum, but that's just how it is sometimes. I pulled her close for a hug. She pushed me away.

"What's the matter?" I asked.

"Stop badgering me!" she squealed.

"But that's what badgers do," I said.

Anyway, I have little tolerance for a woman's tears, much less Bo Peep's as they fall to the floor like grapes off a Napa Valley vine. So of course I took her in my arms and kissed her gently.

"You men!" she kicked me away, uncharacteristically vicious.

"And lucky for you," I responded, suddenly fed up with jousting. "I'm going to bed. You can sleep on the couch or anywhere else that don't fight back."

That is an example of Thursday colliding with Friday (see below, page 95).

An hour later she snuggled in beside me, and before long we were happily coupling. Gnu was in his heaven, and all was right with the world. I woke up singing:

> I see trees of green........ red roses too
> I see em bloom..... for me and for you
> And I think to myself.... what a wonderful world.
>
> I see skies of blue..... clouds of white
> Bright blessed days....dark sacred nights
> And I think to myself .....what a wonderful world.
>
> The colors of a rainbow.....so pretty ..in the sky

Are also on the faces.....of people ..going by

I see friends shaking hands.....sayin. how do you do
They're really sayin......i love you.
I hear babies cry...... I watch them grow
They'll learn much more.....than I'll never know
And I think to myself .....what a wonderful world.[10]

When the alarm rang at 8 a.m., Bo Peep whispered, "I want to sleep in," and disappeared under the covers.

No problem. I slid out of bed to write a book.

****

Dr. Balderdash, my dermatologist, is a cheery little fellow with all his many credentials on display.

Balderdash: Hello McGee, what is it this time?

Well, he has a good memory. I hadn't seen him for two years; then it was to check for melanoma. I was clear.

Badger: Doctor B, I have a little lump beside my right eyelid. Is it my spleen surfacing? A horn? Will I be the first badger unicorn?

Balderdash: Calm down, McGee. Your spleen is a zillion miles away. About unicorns I wouldn't know. Could be ideopathic or iatrogenic.— [i.e., cause unknown or perhaps adverse reactions between drugs.][11] Here, let me have a closer look. Have you been taken by aliens lately? Are you treating this with anything?

Badger: Just my finger. I touch it from time to time to see if it's gone away or become larger. It just keeps growing and getting harder.

---

[10] "What a Wonderful World," lyrics by George David Weiss, George Douglas, Bob Thiel; Ascap.

[11] Iatrogenesis may result from inappropriate medicinal intervention, botched surgery and misdiagnosis in conventional medicine or any alternative therapeutic treatment. (Thanks to Dr. C.T. Wilkes, psychiatrist and Jungian analyst in Calgary, Alberta, for his advice.)

Balderdash: "Ah yes, I see now! It is what we call a Maibomian cyst, a type of chalazion. It is a simple, painless op to remove it and sew up the incision. It will eventually take over your face but otherwise it is benign. There are oral remedies, but I do not favor them. I recommend Traumeel twice a day, if anything. And by the way, the op costs about $3,000, cash on the barrelhead.

Badger: Are you kidding? Surely OHIP covers it.[12] I am insured together with my patron, Master Daemon.

Balderdash: Dear fella, removing benign cysts is considered to be cosmetic surgery, and OHIP does not cover such procedures.

Badger (rising): Very well. Many thanks for your time, Doc. I think I'll just take my chances as a unicorn in Maibomia, where I hear there are pretty lady badgers who do topical.

"Good luck," is all he said.

****

Jazz makes you cooler

Call it cool or modern jazz, the genre pioneered in the early 1970s by Dave Brubeck, Miles Davis, Paul Desmond, Dexter Gordon, Chet Baker, and many others, is Ultima Thule. It is about taking off on a theme or circumambulating a melody, much in the way one comes to an understanding of the images in a dream. Melody is the thread that grounds any rendition of a jazz composition—sax, strings, horns and keyboards may fly off in diverse directions, while percussion (drums, etc.) hold the tension and the bass holds the tempo, anchoring everything, but without the underlying melodic thread, often just out of hearing, it can become simply so much cacophony.

Analogously, the underlying melody in a person's life is her or his values and pattern of living. Dreams are a riff on that melody, and the

---

[12] OHIP=Ontario Health Insurance Plan (i.e., Medicare in Canada).

images in a dream are the high and low notes, the chords. The bass, their essence, holds them to their truth.

I say all this somewhat tentatively, for I am not musically trained, and the analogy may not hold up to close scrutiny, but it feels true to me and worth pondering. Who wants to live a cacaphonic life?

Now, this is a question that didn't occur to me before I spent many wee hours listening to jazz greats and trying to figure out what they were doing and saying. I mean, I didn't know major from minor until the difference was explained to me by my office manager Scott, who moonlights as a professional drummer. Jazz is altogether a mystery to me, but listening to it sure makes me feel good. I enjoy Mozart and Bach too, but they don't stir me viscerally, as do Miles Davis, Dave Brubeck, Charlie Parker and Chet Baker.

All to say, I am in awe of musicians. Daemon once spent a year trying to play the flute, but it turned out that first he had to learn to read music. This utterly defeated him as he fled to Zurich to begin training as a Jungian analyst. Of course, this new direction was a lot more demanding than learning to play the flute, but a much more satisfying endeavor in the long run. Indeed, he says he has learned more from his analysands and from his projections onto lady friends than from anything h was ever taught. That's just how it is when you become conscious of contents in the unconscious hitherto unknown. Not my fault, just the messenger.

Of course, my love of Jung is the underlying melody of my life and this and everything else I have ever written as a grown-up.

****

Consider the following fantasy (call it a chord if you want; it's a free country), conjured up by Daemon's sometime side-kick Razr:

Ann Marie was a cute Irish lass living in the ravine that runs behind Daemon's house. One November day I lured her out of her simple lean-to shelter and brought her home. It was not difficult, for frost was forming on the evergreens, raccoons were scampering about, and she had only a blanket.

After a light snack, some chat and a tour of my house, I invited Ann

Marie to have a nap.

We lay side by side. I tentatively unbuttoned her blouse.

"Would you mind if I explored your body?" I asked.

"You silly, I was hoping you would," replied Ann Marie.

And so I did, and she melted under my fingertips. I caressed and kissed her everywhere. All this sent her into a frenzy, and me too.

Still, I suddenly called a halt.

"Ann Marie," I said, "You are a married woman, and this is as far as I can go."

Ann Marie got up and pulled herself together.

"You are a real bastard," she waved as she left.

I did chew on that, and it was not pleasant.

And where does Jung come into that? Well, my shadow, of course: leading a woman on, to expect more, and unceremoniously turning off my tap of love. And her shadow too, allowing me to drive her to the brink of breaking her marriage vows.

I may be wrong, but I imagine this scenario occurs hundreds of times every day all over the world. Not my fault; I am just the messenger.

Well, it's only a fantasy, one chord among many.

****

The comfort level of the human ear is about 80 decibels. Now, four happy screaming kids under the age of 10 in Daemon's swimming pool generate upwards of 100 decibels—compared to a Harley Davidson motorcycle at 120 and a leaf-blower at 70-80.

My sett is generally quiet as the grave unless I play music, and then I am careful to hold the decibel level to 50-60. Mostly I prefer silence except for the occasional newscasts that only amount to 20-30 decibels.

****

Do not put new butter with old. More people die each year in North America from rancid butter than from AIDS and rabies combined.[13]

And while I'm at it, I'm told by Rebecca that it is unhygienic to cut meat on a wooden chopping block.

---

[13] *American Butter Board advisory,* May, 2013.

****

Now, take corn. Corn is very nutritious; it has all the vitamins you can think of, and niacin and fiber as well as calories.

But popcorn, now that's a different thing. Popcorn has zero calories and all the nutrients have been plumb popped out into the air. You get something if you add butter and salt, but then you're into fat and more calories than you need on the couch or in the movie theater.

I have written deep and deeper about Jungian psychology from the standpoint of Logos, and I am now more interested in writing from an Eros perspective—irrational, whimsical, joyful—my experience of individuation rather than what I've read it's supposed to look like. Although I tread in Jung's footsteps, I do not reach his bootstraps.

****

I recently terminated analysis with a young (40sh) man after three years. He had often said he longed for an epiphany. And finally he had one—he realized he no longer needed me.

This young man had changed more than he realized; from drawing an elephant curled up in an eggplant he had graduated to building small pagodas to welcome and safeguard his spirit gods, as the Japanese traditionally do (btw, his wife is Japanese).

Well, I can't do better than that. An analyst who says she or he can is either asleep or inflated.

It is official doctrine for analysts not to accept gifts from their analysands. But in my final session with this young man, when he presented me with a miniature pagoda, I received it in tears. A Logos orientation would see this exchange in terms of transference and countertransference, and that's not exactly untrue, but I accepted it in the spirit of Eros.

****

Call me a Luddite, but I do not participate in social media like Facebook, Twitter, Linked-in, etc. The Internet is a useful medium for e-mail, and I have my time full of that already, and so I eschew social media in favor of sleeping until noon or reading a book.

****

A new year and Christmas approaches. I am hardly ready, but I am glad to be still standing despite my aches and pains. Well, however you cut it, aging is not a bed of roses. But to perk you up, read Dr. Seuss, *You're Only Old Once.*

I am not a practicing Christian. However, I still love to hear the traditional Christmas carols I absorbed in the Regina United Church Sunday School basement some 70 years ago. They hit me in the gut as I enjoyed Bingo with my gramma and she fed me hot dogs and pop. That is possibly the origin of my subsequent dissolute life.

****

I am now up late, Scotch in hand, listening to Frank Sinatra's album, *Songs for Swinging Lovers.* This is rather masochistic of me, since my lover is elsewhere, so I am not swinging, but I do so enjoy Frank's voice and the way he twists it around lyrics that make my heart swell. Everything he sings, at no matter his age, evokes my youthful exploits. He makes me feel young again and dissolves my current woes. This is worth a lot to me in my solitary sett or turret.

I am told by a friend that Pluto is currently transiting my Venus, which apparently foreshadows emotional turmoil. Yes, that is happening in my life, and it is why I revert to Ol' Blue Eyes. He is candy for the troubled soul. Well, arguably more healthy than Oreo cookies or Ritz biscuits.

I can't do music here, but I can give you some lyrics that may remind you of your past passions and long for more to come:

> You're just too marvelous, too marvelous for words
> Like glorious, glamorous and that old standby amorous
> It's all too wonderful, I'll never find the words
> That say enough, tell enough, I mean they just aren't swell enough
>
> You're much too much and just too very, very
> To ever be in Webster's Dictionary
> And so I'm borrowing a love song from the birds
> To tell you that you're marvelous, too marvelous for words
>
> You're much, you're too much and just too very, very

29

To ever be, to ever be in Webster's Dictionary
And so I'm borrowing a love song from the birds
To tell you that you're marvelous, tell you that you're marvelous
Tell you that you're marvelous, too marvelous for words.[14]

****

Here's to you, 'cause jazz makes you cooler.

****

I was recently presented with a dilemma when an analysand urged me to see his wife for a few hours. That prompted quite a conflict in me. On the one hand I wanted to meet her, a woman he described as beautiful, intelligent, well-read in Jungian psychology and interested in getting to know me. On the other hand, my analytic task was to get to know his inner life through his eyes and his unconscious; to be presented with the reality of his outer life would certainly confuse me. I saw it as a boundary issue, and after thoughtful consideration I had to refuse his request.

Of course, I would have discussed all this with him in our next session, particularly why he was so keen for me to see his wife. This might have revealed at lot going on in him under the surface, and led to a fruitful dialogue between us. That is what analytic work is all about. However, he chose not to see me again.

****

I am reading Lucretius' ancient work, *On the Nature of Things,* in spite of what I might otherwise be doing or reading or writing. It happened by accident. I heard an interview on CBC radio with Stephen Greenblatt about his book, *The Swerve: How the World Became Modern.* I immediately ordered this book from the library, and had it in hand a few days later. This led me in turn to Lucretius' mentor Epicurus, and I've been going back and forth between them for many days.

Let me tell you: Lucretius' lengthy prose-poem is almost impossible to understand (at least in English translation), except that he

---

[14] Sinatra, "Too Marvelous," music and lyrics by Richard Whiting and Johnny Mercer; Ascap.

champions Epicurus's tenets about atomism (everything is made of little bits) and the pursuit of pleasure—a quest displaced for two centuries by Catholic Christianity promoting the pursuit of pain as the path to salvation; e.g., by self-flagellation, self-denial and the like. Indeed, according to current scholarship, not much is known about Epicurus except what Lucretius wrote about his teachings. All this is quite baffling to me, for I am not a scholar. I am a simple-minded badger and otherwise out of my depth.

Now, in our enlightened twenty-first century, we are apt to forget the power wielded by the Roman Catholic Church in the Middle Ages, as evinced for instance by the Inquisition, rampant accusations against women for witchcraft, and the burning at the stake of Joan of Arc. Catholicism currently seems to be on the decline, and to my mind the world would be a better place without its *ex cathedra* declarations.

According to Greenblatt, Thomas Jefferson, one of the writers of the U.S. Declaration of Independence, put his stamp on the new republic in endorsing Lucretius' and Epicurus' ideas by including in the Declaration the injunction that the government's role was not only to secure the lives and liberties of its citizens, but also to serve "the pursuit of happiness." This is the idea of "atomism" at work in the real world. Greenblatt writes:

On August 15, 1820, the seventy-seven-year-old Jefferson wrote to another former president, his friend John Adams. Adams was eighty-five, and the two old men were in the habit of exchanging views on the meaning of life, as they felt it ebb away. "I [am] obliged to recur ultimately to my habitual anodyne, Jefferson wrote":

"I feel, therefore I exist. I feel bodies which are not myself: there are other existencies then. I call them *matter.* I feel them changing place. This gives me *motion.* Where there is an absence of matter, I call it *void,* or *nothing,* or *immaterial space.* On the basis of sensation, of matter and motion, we may erect the fabric of all the certainties we can have or need."

These are the sentiments that Lucretius had most hoped to instill in his readers. "I am," Jefferson wrote to a correspondent who wanted to know his philosophy of life, "an Epicurean."[15]

Thassall for now. The little ones are waiting for a bedtime story, and I know Daemon is dying to have a say. See you around, or a square.

****

By the way, I confess that parts of this chapter were written by Daemon. He is the analyst; I am but his foil, and it isn't always easy to tell the difference. I am all in a muddle. Ambiguity and paradox may be our downfall.

And speaking of puppets, I am one, and the puppeteer, of course, is the Self.

Drawing by Leigh Hobbs in *Mr. Badger and the Magic Mirror.*

---

[15] Stephen Greenblatt, *The Swerve: How the World Became Modern,* p. 263.

2
DAEMON ONE
All About Shadow

Well, every badger has his day, but let's get down to serious business.

> The shadow is a moral problem that challenges the whole ego-personality,
> for no one can become conscious of the shadow without considerable
> moral effort. To become conscious of it involves recognizing the dark as-
> pects of the personality as present and real. This act is the essential condi-
> tion for any kind of self-knowledge, and it therefore, as a rule, meets with
> considerable resistance. Indeed, self-knowledge as a psychotherapeutic
> measure frequently requires much painstaking work extending over a long
> period. [16]

You can say that again: "Self-knowledge requires much painstaking
work extending over a long period"—indeed, more or less forever.

Alas, people seeking relief from psychic distress generally want and
expect a quick fix. Hence the rise of such disciplines as "short-term psychotherapy," "mindfulness" and "behavior modification," all with a focus on alleviating symptoms asap. These are fine and good as far as they
go in reducing suffering, but they leave untouched the underlying factors
that plague the whole personality and which may unexpectedly erupt
again, willy-nilly. Above all, they tend to ignore the pervasive influence
of the unconscious in the overall psychic economy. Jung writes:

> The archetypes most clearly characterized from the empirical point of
> view are those which have the most frequent and the most disturbing in-
> fluence on the ego. These are the *shadow,* the *anima,* and the *animus.* [17]

Elsewhere I have dealt at length with the latter two, the so-called contrasexual archetypes/complexes. [18] Here we will consider Jung's views on

---

[16] "The Shadow," *Aion,* CW 9ii, par. 14. (CW refers throughout to *The Collected Works
of C. G. Jung.)*

[17] Ibid., par. 13.

[18] See "The Syzygy: Anima and Animus," in Sharp, *Jung Uncorked,* Book Two, pp. 10ff.

how the shadow is related, in a compensatory way, to the one-sided attitudes of ego-consciousness.

Emotional discomfort is a hallmark of the shadow. Whenever something we have done, are doing, or think of doing causes us to feel guilty, ashamed, embarrassed or dumb, we can be sure the shadow side of the personality is involved. The shadow is by definition the polar opposite of the bright, intelligent, honorable and morally responsible persona with which the ego tends to identify.

I must back up a little here, to remind the reader that the persona is a complex primarily conditioned by culture and environment. It is the aspect of ourselves that we generally show to others—charming, enlightened, tolerant and socially acceptable. It is both a mask and a defense, at times helpful and necessary, but not who we really are.

The persona aims to live up to what is expected, what is "proper." It is a useful bridge socially and an indispensable protective covering; without a persona, we are simply too vulnerable to the outside world. We regularly cover up inferiorities with a persona, since we do not like our weaknesses to be seen. As well, civilized society depends on interactions between people through the persona. But it is psychologically unhealthy to identify with it, to believe we are "nothing but" the person we show to others.

Generally speaking, the shadow is less civilized, more primitive, cares little for social propriety. What is of value to the persona is anathema to the shadow, and vice versa. Hence the shadow and the persona function in a compensatory way: the brighter the light, the darker the shadow. The more one identifies with the persona—which in effect is to deny that one has a shadow—the more trouble one will have with the unacknowledged other side of the personality, which may unexpectedly put us to shame.

Thus the shadow constantly challenges the morality of the persona, and, to the extent that ego-consciousness identifies with the persona, the shadow also threatens the ego. In the process of psychological development that Jung called individuation, disidentification from the persona and the conscious assimilation of the shadow go hand in hand. The ideal is to have an ego strong enough to acknowledge both the persona and the shadow without identifying with either.

In this day and age, the notion of a persona is pretty well understood, though it may soon be overtaken by the term "avatar," traditionally a spiritual guide but now common in the so-called metaverse (metaphorical, virtual universes like Second Life and Facebook) or dating sites on the Internet. Indeed, one's avatar in this sense may simply personify one's shadow, or at least as much of it as one is comfortable revealing to strangers.

Psychologically speaking, the shadow is everywhere—behind the scenes like the phantom of the opera, the fly in the ointment, the skeleton in the closet. There is nothing too nefarious for the shadow to have a hand in—tax evasion, extramarital affairs, fraud, arson, spousal and child abuse, rape, murder, religious and political strife, and on and on. In short, *the shadow is everywhere.* That is the inescapable reality behind Jung's oft-quoted admonition:

> We need more psychology. We need more understanding of human nature, because the only real danger that exists is man himself. He is the great danger, and we are pitifully unaware of it. We know nothing of man, far too little. His psyche should be studied, because we are the origin of all coming evil.[19]

There is no way to escape the insidious influence of the shadow except to become conscious of it. To be aware of what we are capable of does not make us invulnerable, but it can prepare us for the unexpected scenarios of life. A harmless flirtation can escalate; a few juggled figures can land us in jail. That is the shadow at work.

But hold your horses. The shadow is not all bad news. Besides unacceptable impulses, repressed or suppressed, the shadow may also contain ignored or forgotten potential. I mean to say, the shadow can be a destructive influence, but it may also be creative. That is one essential difference between Jung's view of the unconscious and that of Freud, who saw the unconscious (or "id") as entirely negative, a repository of

---

[19] "The 'Face to Face' Interview," 1959, in William McGuire and R. F. C. Hull, eds. *C. G. Jung Speaking: Interviews and Encounters*, p. 436.

repressed childhood sexual desires.

I think of Jocelyn, a feisty thirty-year-old, underpaid and overworked as a "gofer" in the film industry. She had barely finished high school and felt trapped in her situation without more education. She came to me with the following dream:

> Where am I? On a cloud?! Yes, I am floating high above the earth with the wings of an angel. An elegant gentleman approaches and hands me a cap and gown. "You forgot these," he says.

Well I can tell you I was nearly overcome with delight. Jocelyn was wary; she had not yet come to trust the imagery of her dreams. I saw the "elegant gentleman" as a helpful animus figure, and encouraged her to think of going back to school. A few months later she enrolled in a pre-university make-up course, and within a year she was accepted into a Bachelor of Arts program in literature. She thanked me. I bowed to her unconscious.

The shadow has a mercurial quality—it assumes different shapes in its hosts. In a chemistry lab, touch a blob of the silvery element mercury and it breaks into pieces that scurry off in all directions. That is what the shadow does, mercurial, putting us at odds with ourselves, or leading us along a new path.

****

Ah, the girls of summer are out again, at last. How I love to see the colorful swirly frocks, the short shorts and skimpy halter tops, the barely-contained bouncing tops and bottoms. It is the anticipation of these comely sights that makes the icy Canadian winter almost bearable. Many men look forward to baseball's so-called boys of summer, but I am all for the feminine mystique as it manifests in pent-up female urges joyfully to display their barely-veiled erotic charms. Die-hard feminists don't like to admit that such attire is intrinsically provocative, but it obviously is. Perhaps they are just too young or uneducated to know what the word provocative means; e.g., suggestive, stimulating, etc. I mean, men instinctively ogle semi-clad women passing by on the street.

Not my fault, just the messenger.

36

Okay, so I may be an elderly daemon or badger, suit yourself, but I am not a eunuch. And I have an abiding interest in fashion.

To be clear, I love women and respect them.

Men's voyeurism may be judged salacious on the one hand, but on the other, accepted by fair-minded folks as a natural concomitant of the animal condition and an integral aspect of the human psyche as it has evolved to perpetuate the race. It is true that I am "only human," but you get my drift.

Oh, the innocence of adolescent girls not yet aware of the power they will later wield over men by virtue of having a cleavage and a yoni. The Greek courtesan Lysistrata could be their model. In 425 B.C. she urged her sisters to withhold sex from their warrior mates until they signed a treaty ending the Peloponnesian War, the fabled battle between nation-states Athens and Sparta (431-404 B.C.). As it happens, her strategy did not work, for the women themselves were too lustful to abstain, and so the wars continued for another twenty years.[20]

So sue me for appreciating the feminine as it crosses my path. I have letters from many mature female readers applauding the views expressed on this subject in my previous books—inviting closer contact, cohabitation even. And some pretty ladies, otherwise chaste, have been known to come awry in my presence, just for the fun of it.

Well, these are projections that I am hard pressed not to take advantage of. Yes, now and then I may slip up but I am not invulnerable, and it's evolution. Get used to it.

Night has fallen, and there's nothing we can do about it. I long for bed, but how to tear myself away from Stan Getz playing "Misty"? That is the question.

> Look at me
> I'm as helpless as a kitten up a tree
> And I feel like I'm clinging to a cloud
> I can't understand
> I get misty, just holding your hand

---

[20] This is all according to the comic play, *Lysistrata,* by Aristophanes, first performed in 411 B.C.

Walk my way
And a thousand violins begin to play
Or it might be the sound of your hello
That music I hear
I get misty the moment you're near

You can say that you're leading me on
But it's just what I want you to do
Don't you notice how hopelessly I'm lost
That's why I'm following you

On my own
Would I wander through this wonderland alone
Never knowing my right foot from my left
My hat from my glove
I'm too misty and too much in love.[21]

****

I seldom think about the past, and I do not worry about the future. What is left? Well, I am focused on expressing what occupies my mind in the present—what is right in front of me. There are a multitude of issues I could bring to the fore, ego-concerns, but I hesitate to mention the obvious and the trivial, which both alike bore me stupid.

So saying, I want to bring my mother into this narrative. This may seem odd or inappropriate, even goofy, but I will tell you how it came about.

Some weeks ago I plucked *War and Peace* off the library shelf, having convinced myself that it was time to read Tolstoy. Well, I stuck with it for 150 pages (out of 700) and finally gave up. What a turgid mess of potage: aristocratic buffoonery, military arrogance, coquettish ladies with wide-open bodices but lower regions veiled by stylish beaded reticules (whatever they were) and minds occupied by gossip and the latest fad at court. I mean I had to wonder why this book has been deemed a "classic," though I concede that I was simply not prepared for its sweep and grandeur. (I have since seen the opera, which I enjoyed.)

---

[21] Lyrics and music by Johnny Burke, Erroll Garner/ © Warner/Chappell Music, Inc.

I turned instead to Carol Shields' *The Stone Diaries,* which I had started some time ago but laid aside, not then ready for the candid, open-hearted recounting of a woman's life in many different voices, including, of course, her shadowy thoughts, which now quite bowled me over. I became completely engaged with this Pulitzer Prize winner.

In the midst of this enchantment I dreamed of my mother, who died some twenty years ago and who has not since weighed heavily in my thoughts until I became seriously engrossed in this essay and writing this book.

I recall my mother, née Marion Weist, as a stereotypical woman of the 1930s, 40s and 50s. Her peasant parents had immigrated to Canada in the 1880s from a German-speaking enclave in Odessa, then known as "White Russia" (now part of Ukrainia). My gramma Weist never learned to read or write English, but her husband, Martin by name, became literate enough to land a job as a typesetter on the *Regina Leader Post* newspaper. They anchored a happy extended family in Regina, prairie capital of Saskatchewan in western Canada.

Among my fondest memories are Sunday dinners with them all, followed by polka dancing or bingo, canasta, euchre or poker. My gramma knew her numbers very well and made sure I did too. Or else we took turns on the Ouija board or reading tea leaves, which is a whole other story from my shadowy past, best saved for the novel I'll never write. My gramma's folklore wisdom began and ended with the mantra, "Never put anything in your ear but your elbow." She was fat, loving and always jolly, except for the time her twenty-five-year-old daughter Eva (my mom's younger sister) died from a botched tonsillectomy. Gramma took to her bed and cried for four whole days. I have never since heard of such keening except among primitive tribes. I was seven at the time and didn't really know what was happening, but I was lost in the family grief.

My mother was the kind of woman portrayed in television sitcoms of the period—selfless, modest, unassuming, guileless, completely devoted to husband and two smart-ass sons who teased her unmercifully. She clipped recipes from the *Reader's Digest* and *Ladies Home Companion,* and gave me what for if I didn't finish my breakfast porridge or came home late from school. She had been a chorus-line dancer before wedding my father in 1932, but that oomph was gone by the time I became sentient. Except, however, I do recall one night when my father, then a corporal in the Royal Canadian Air Force, came home plastered, and in a snit she tore all the buttons off his uniform. I remember too that she sewed them back on in the morning before he left. And polished his boots.

That's the kind of wife she was, and very pretty too—not Garbo or Dietrich seductive, more like the laid-back, mild-mannered Lillian Gish. In my waiting room there hangs a picture of my mom with two-year-old me on her lap. I adored my mother, and as a kid I used to creep up behind her and untie her apron strings, just to see her woop with joy. I wore her chorus girl outfit on Halloween until I was twelve. "Leave the dishes in the sink, Ma" was a song written to give her a break from unrelenting domestic chores, about which she never complained. In those Great Depression years, money was always tight, and I was six years old before she took me to the local soda fountain for a special treat—my first taste of ice cream. A Freudian might have a field day with all that—wrap it in a neat Oedipal bow, but I accept it as a just-so story.

Okay, so I have a mother complex. And who has not? Only now, in my senior years, do I wonder what my mom's inner life was like. Oh, I do feel badly about my neglect of her! My heart aches and I am ashamed to realize how I took her affectionate concern for granted and never wondered who was there behind it. You see, her life was lived on a persona level, always for others. Whatever personal potential she had—let's call it her shadow in this context—never came to light, and I never gave her unlived life a thought. Shame on me.

****

Tonight, alone in my turret, I fell in love with Janis Joplin, again. The first time was during a few days in a Victorian house in San Francisco near Haight-Ashbury, 1971, when I sat stoned in the living room going crazy listening on a ghetto-blaster to her last album, *Pearl* (including

"Cry Baby," "Me and Bobby McGee," and "Piece of My Heart.")

Janis Joplin, husky-voiced singer/composer, was all heart, and above all, *real*. She sang as if berserk and joyfully gyrated on stage like a Dionysian maenad. Many of her memorable performances are available on YouTube. She looks so cute and cuddly, shoulder-length hair flying, you'd never guess she came from a straight-laced family, parents in the business world. She was more or less disowned by her provincial home town of Port Arthur in Texas, though she credited it for her creative roots. She rose to fame in spite of her reluctance to be a rock star. It just happened as she rode the rebellious wave of the 1960s, the first genuine female rock and blues icon, adored and applauded by millions. And yet she often confessed that she felt so lonely….

In one of her last talks with an old high-school friend who asked her after a performance, "What's it like to live a rock-star life? Janis replied, "This is no way to live a life," and earlier, in an interview with a German television station, she said, "There will always be the bulk of people out there who are straight." And by "straight" she didn't mean drug-free, but those who live according to prevailing collective values. So she put herself on the line by creating her own path, eventually tragic, but still, she was her own woman in the midst of a crazy-making music industry that sought to make fortunes by controlling the careers of their popular artists. She was an original. If not the greatest singer of her generation, she was arguably the most passionately determined to be herself.

Janis Joplin's death in 1970 is still somewhat of a mystery. She was found by her manager alone in a hotel room, apparently dead from a heroin overdose, though she had been clean for the previous six months and had a lot to look forward to as she finished recording *Pearl*, and was engaged to a fellow musician. She was just 27 years old, an age when many other Greats were visited by Death (e.g. Amy Winehouse, Jim Morrison, Jimi Hendrix, Kurt Cobain, etc., and see the film *Meet Joe Black*).

Back then, in 1971, not knowing she had died a year before, it was impossible for a man like me (i.e., one with a savior complex) not to want to hold and protect this beautiful, vulnerable creature (like Mimi in *La Bohème)* and it still is. You will pardon me for being a romantic, which you knew already anyway. Well, we don't outlive our complexes; we only get used to them.

So here's one of my Janis favorites:

Oh, come on, come on, come on, come on

Didn't I make you feel like you were the only man - yeah!
An' didn't I give you nearly everything that a woman possibly can?
Honey, you know I did!
And each time I tell myself that I, well I think I've had enough,
But I'm gonna show you, baby, that a woman can be tough.

I want you to come on, come on, come on, come on and take it,
Take it!
Take another little piece of my heart now, baby!
Oh, oh, break it!
Break another little bit of my heart now, darling, yeah, yeah, yeah.
Oh, oh, have a!
Have another little piece of my heart now, baby,
You know you got it if it makes you feel good,
Oh, yes indeed.

You're out on the streets looking good,
And baby deep down in your heart
I guess you know that it ain't right,
Never, never, never, never, never, never hear me when I cry at night,
Baby, and I cry all the time!
But each time I tell myself that I, well I can't stand the pain,
But when you hold me in your arms, I'll sing it once again.

I'll say come on, come on, come on, come on and take it!
Take it!
Take another little piece of my heart now, baby.
Oh, oh, break it!
Break another little bit of my heart now, darling, yeah,
Oh, oh, have a!
Have another little piece of my heart now, baby,
You know you got it, child, if it makes you feel good.

I need you to come on, come on, come on, come on and take it,
Take it!
Take another little piece of my heart now, baby!
Oh, oh, break it!
Break another little bit of my heart, now darling, yeah, c'mon now.
Oh, oh, have a

Have another little piece of my heart now, baby.
You know you got it - whoahhhhh!!

Take it!
Take it! Take another little piece of my heart now, baby,
Oh, oh, break it!
Break another little bit of my heart, now darling, yeah, yeah, yeah,
yeah,
Oh, oh, have a
Have another little piece of my heart now, baby, hey,
You know you got it, child, if it makes you feel good.[22]

An analyst/friend suggests that it is regressive at my age to treasure a sexy, self-destructive young rock-star. That may be true, but what the hell, I know the difference between an anima figure and a real woman. I can love them both, dispensing Eros as needed, with no conflict between them or in me.

Dear reader, how often must it be said, again and again, that love is the answer to many of life's sorrows? Love can even compensate for an apparently meaningless work life, and according to recent statistics, 80% of working men and women in North America do not enjoy their jobs.[23]

Our collective Western culture touts success and upward mobility. The truth is that those on the bottom rung of the success ladder are stuck there indefinitely. Now I ask you, what is left for them but acceptance of their plight and the pursuit of love?

Of course, however you cut it, love (a basket word for feelings) is a gamble and a mystery, and often a disaster. But life is boring and un-grounded without a loving connection to a companionable other.

Get used to it—the world is not your oyster, but rather a clamshell. You have much to give. Look around: there are others who feel equally alone, needing someone to love and be loved by. So give your all and hope for the best.

Not my fault, just the messenger.

****

---

[22] "Piece of My Heart," lyrics by Janis; on *Pearl,* Columbia Records; Ascap.

[23] Ecko-Wright Polls, *Toronto Mirror,* February 2013.

Note this cynical remark by Nietzsche:

> Woman would like to believe that love can achieve *everything*—it is her
> characteristic superstition. Alas, whoever knows the heart will guess how
> poor, helpless, arrogant and mistaken is even the best, the profoundest,
> love,—how it even destroys rather than saves.[24]

I generally like Nietzsche, but I am not so pessimistic. I am a Romantic. I
believe in love and its redemptive potential, for I have experienced it and
watched it happen in others. Take El Jay now. I was wanting someone to
love, and she appeared at my door. That's what my tribe calls synchronicity, a meaningful coincidence.

It is true that in my youth I was a foot-loose, fancy-free *puer*—about
which I have written more than enough—but all that was before El Jay
somewhat tentatively approached me declaring an appreciation of Inner
City Books and especially my own writing. I claim she seduced me, but
she feels otherwise; this difference of opinion simply amuses us.

Anyway, I fell for El Jay head over heels as she tamed me to become
only hers. We have been together now for many honeymoon years, but
my early footloose life continues to intrigue me. Paris, London, Rome,
Zurich, Prague, Rome, Corfu. I stumbled through them all, scathed but
still standing. I ended up back in Toronto, which is the perfect place for
me—multicultural, friendly, close to my children and snooker dens, jazz
and film festivals, no unwelcome demands. I have my turret on the second floor, badger in his sett in the basement, and an ensuiteheart for El
Jay on the third floor when she visits.

Mine is essentially a lonely life, but it suits my temperament, and I can
venture into the collective on my own terms, which is typically to shop
for groceries or make deliveries on my walker for "Meals on Wheels."

****

I am familiar enough with the masculine shadow, but I can hardly fathom
the other side of women, which to this day bemuses me. Of course, this
does not prevent me from loving them to pieces. Come to think of it,

---

[24] "Nietzsche Contra Wagner," in *The Portable Nietzsche,* p. 679.

when I was growing up, not a day would pass when I didn't hear my father tell my mother he loved her, at which she beamed. They were a model of a happy, solid relationship. Symbiotic, perhaps, but what happy relationship is not if you look closely enough?

As I have said elsewhere, I like living alone, but a loving woman trumps solitude. However, more to the point here, it is the mysterious, shadowy spark that ignites a woman's desire for intimacy that puzzles and eludes me. I am not even sure if that spark is properly described as "shadowy"; it may be an expression of her essence, for all I know. But I can hardly count the number of women in my practice who have confided their physical indifference to mates and lust for someone else. Only the messenger.

My ignorance of the female shadow is only mitigated these days by the tender confidences of my consort El Jay and those women brave enough to reveal themselves in art, song or books. Off the top of my head I think of Virginia Woolf, Billie Holiday, Janis Joplin, Grace Slick, Stevie Nicks, Sylvia Plath, Willa Cather, Alice Munroe, Carol Shields of course, Barbra Streisand, Tina Turner, Madonna, and don't forget Emily Dickinson. Go ahead; compile your own list of shadow-conscious women. I dare say there are and have been thousands, mostly unsung outside their immediate family or circle of friends.

In practice, as noted often in this series, the shadow and everything associated with it is virtually synonymous with unlived life. "There must be more to life than this," is a remark heard often enough in the consulting room. And it is true. All that I consciously am and aspire to be effectively shuts out what I might be, could be, *also am*. Some of what I "also am" has been repressed because it was or is unacceptable to oneself or others, and some is simply unrealized potential—none of it easy to differentiate.

Of course, in my analytic practice I come across people with absent or negative mothers. Unless I can establish a degree of rapport with such clients, who are often tied up inside with resentment, bitterness, abandonment and a pervasive desire for revenge, I am useless to them, for my approach to life's dilemmas is not as a soothsayer or spiritual director or hit man. I am someone who accompanies those individuals on the path they intuit for themselves. Though I may on occasion give a prod or two, I cannot save people from themselves. This is as much as I can say about my analytic "technique," which in fact is simply an attitude that takes the unconscious seriously. And this may go on for months or even years, until the client says something like, "Thanks Doc, it's been real and un-real; I think I can manage now on my own" (and I am not even a doctor).

Through introspection, we can become aware of shadow aspects of our own personality, but we may still resist them or fear their influence. And even where they are known and would be welcome, they are not readily available to the conscious will. For instance, my intuition may be shadowy—primitive and unadapted—so I cannot call it up when it's needed. I may know that feeling is required in a particular situation but for the life of me can't muster it. I want to enjoy the party but my care-free extraverted side has vanished. I may know I'm due for some intro-version, but the lure of the bright lights is just too strong.

The shadow does not necessarily demand equal time with the ego, but for a balanced personality it does require recognition. For the introvert this may involve an occasional night on the town—against his "better judgment." For the extravert it might involve—in spite of herself—an evening staring at the wall.

In general, the person whose shadow is repressed gives the impression of being dull and stodgy. This is particularly evident in a man's attitude toward women. The loyal, persona-identified man ignores or suppresses his instinctive reactions to females other than his partner. The shadow-conscious man accepts and enjoys the reality that his psyche is host to a harem of lovely ladies, while being wary of acting on his errant erotic impulses. On the whole, I think a man's women friends appreciate this as a measure of his character—though it may be something one recognizes but does not say out loud.

On the other hand, nowadays I have heard it called "emotional infidel-ity" when a man or woman has a close other-gender friend. What non-sense, I say! Enjoy the happiness that spills over to all. Of course, one's partner may have his or her own insecurities, but that is another story that

I will not explore here.

Needless to say, this is a man-centric view of male-female relationships. Women can write their own books if they have the heart for it.

For a man to be in love after an intimate encounter is so generally known that it hardly bears mentioning. Not so widely known is that this feeling is often tinged with more than a touch of gratitude for having been received back into the source, as it were, safely enveloped by the warm embrace of the Great Mother. More than one besotted man has married the apparent hostess of such "oceanic" feelings—and not always to his or her regret, divorce rates notwithstanding.

The vagina, with its fascinating folds and ravines, is an inexhaustibly rich mystery to a man. It is also a woman's not-so-secret weapon in the battle of the sexes. Pudendum trumps phallus any day, perhaps because of that oceanic feeling it elicits in a man when he penetrates, and vice versa, for all I know. These body parts, however, are not impersonal; they have character and integrity. That is why rape is such a traumatic violation of self. Straight-talking analyst Albert Kreinheder describes the vulva as "a cushioned, silky, fleecy place, springy like a tiger's paw, slippery and gorged with blood, inviting my entry."[25] Well, that is about as far as you can get from the legendary fantasy of the fearsome *vagina dentata* (toothed vagina).[26]

It is widely believed that it is essentially hormonic harmony that fuels romantic fantasies, and that may be so. Love at first sight happens often enough and I have heard of love at first hug too. But it is not common knowledge that emotional reactions toward others are rooted in one's personal psychology and may have little to do with the other person. This is due to the phenomenon of projection, whereby we see in others unconscious aspects of ourselves—traits or qualities we are aware of only dimly, if at all. Listen to what men say or sing about women: "You've captured my soul," "Can't live without you," and so on—and pity the poor woman who is prey to these sentiments and falls for them without a grain

---

[25] *Body and Soul,* p. 45.

[26] The Austrian psychoanalyst Otto Rank first identified this image in 1924, in his book *The Trauma of Birth,* as a widespread cause of anxiety among neurotic men.

of salt. Now don't get me wrong. I am entirely in favor of projection in the service of life and love. Love is naturally blind, but there is a limit.

Projection is a fact of life. We do not consciously make projections; we meet with them. In Jung's pithy sentence, "Projections change the world into the replica of one's own unknown face."[27] We are powerless when in the grip of a projection, good or bad, and we rarely comprehend what hit us. Alas, as Jung was wont to emphasize, the unconscious *is* unconscious. All the same, in the Jungian world we are not foolish enough to speak of projections unless there are obvious problems in a relationship. We do not stir a pot that isn't boiling over, and who among us is fit to discern "true love" from projection? It's a mug's game. But as I said, I am one hundred percent in favor of projection that fuels romance. Indeed, it will be my downfall, if not already.

But what, you may ask, does romance have to do with the shadow? Well, that is a fair question.

I think that all most fellas really need to be happy is "a kiss to build a dream on." In other words, a little show of Eros is all it takes to get the fantasy mill churning. This is a man's fundamental reality, though he may fudge it with scholarly or jocular talk. A woman's reality is unknown to me, but possibly similar, except for the jock talk, though I'm not even sure of that.

I mean, you gotta be pretty cynical to think love is *just* an illusion. It is often that, of course, but hardly the whole story.

Jung noted that the opposite of love is not hate, but power.[28] However, that still leaves a lot of nuances to be accounted for: power for what purpose, love of what and who and why? Such reflections can easily lead to a miasma of doubt and conflict, which as a matter of fact is good for the soul but not often a happy time for the ego.

Come to think of it, maybe cynicism is also the flip side of love; which is to say that someone who is cynical, world-weary, is ripe for falling in love. It is hard to find any man, or woman, at any age, who fell in love with a blank slate. There is always a hook (something in the other

---

[27] "The Shadow," *Aion,* CW 9ii, par. 17.

[28] *Two Essays,* CW 7, par. 78.

that elicits a certain passion), and an ineluctable draw toward fulfilling one's personal destiny, articulated or not.

I think of my client Roger, so delighted one night by his wife's enthusiastic response to him, that he said, "You aren't always like this; what's up?" She threw him out of bed and he charged her with assault. They later divorced, to no one's surprise but his.

Well, there's only one way out of this cul de sac—a little song and dance. How about this:

> You made me love you
> I didn't want to do it, I didn't want to do it
> You made me love you and all the time you knew it
> I guess you always knew it.
> You made me happy sometimes, you made me glad
> But there were times, dear, you made me feel so bad
>
> You made me sigh for, I didn't want to tell you
> I didn't want to tell you
> I want some love that's true, yes I do, deed I do, you know I do
> Give me, give me, give me what I cry for
> You know you got the brand of kisses that I'd die for
> You know you made me love you.[29]

Some years ago, gripped by midnight madness, I offered to give a seminar for the local Jungian community called "The Love Syndrome." It was duly scheduled for a year ahead and registrations poured in, but after sober thought I canceled the event. It just seemed too pretentious, and I quailed at the prospect of having to contain so many complexes.

Now, there are those who eschew romance on account of potential suffering. I am aware of such concerns—having been there myself—but nonetheless I pursue romance at every turn. Knock me down and I get up, and fall right over again. Sinatra swings it gently like this:

> Moon River, wider than a mile
> I'm crossing you in style someday
> You dream maker, you heartbreaker

---

[29] "You Made Me Love You," made popular by Al Jolson, Judy Garland, Doris Day, Patsy Cline and others; music by James V. Monaco, lyrics by Joseph McCarthy; Ascap.

Wherever you're going I'm going your way

Two drifters off to see the world
There's such a lot of world to see
We're after the same rainbows end
Waiting round the bend
My huckleberry friend, Moon River
And me.[30]

The simple truth is that I would rather be in love than in charge. And my shadow agrees with that.

****

It is well known that Jung was both appreciative and critical of the Christian ethic.[31] In terms of the shadow, this is nowhere more evident than in the following letter he wrote to a young Christian woman, referring to the words of Jesus in Mathew 25:

I admire Christians,
Because when you see someone who is hungry or thirsty,
You see Jesus.
When you welcome a stranger, someone who is "strange,"
You welcome Jesus.
When you clothe someone who is naked, you clothe Jesus.
What I do not understand, however,
Is that Christians never seem to recognize Jesus
In their own poverty.
You always want to do good to the poor outside you
And at the same time you deny the poor person
Living inside you.
Why can't you see Jesus in your own poverty,
In your own hunger and thirst?
In all that is "strange" inside you:
In the violence and the anguish that are beyond your control!

---

[30] "Moon River," from *Frank Sinatra: Romance,* music and lyrics by Henry Mancini and Johnny Mercer; BMI.

[31] See John P. Dourley, *The Illness That We Are: A Jungian Critique of Christianity,* esp. chap. 1, "Jung's Ambivalence Toward Christianity," pp. 7ff.

> You are called to welcome all this, not *to deny* its existence,
> But to accept that it is there and to meet Jesus there.[32]

Well, no wonder Jung wrote an extensive piece on "Christ, a Symbol of the Self,"[33] which I commend to all those seeking a bridge between their atheistic beliefs and Christianity. From a psychological perspective, they are compensatory shadow concepts. If you cannot acknowledge that, you might wisely consider personal analysis.

Love Day

Well, this being Valentine's Day, and love in the air, I can't resist the impulse to end this chapter with the familiar song written to pluck our heart strings:

> Behold the way our fine feathered friend,
> His virtue doth parade
> Thou knowest not, my dim-witted friend
> The picture thou hast made
> Thy vacant brow, and thy tousled hair
> Conceal thy good intent
> Thou noble upright truthful sincere,
> And slightly dopey gent
>
> You're my funny valentine,
> Sweet comic valentine,
> You make me smile with my heart.
> Your looks are laughable, un-photographable,
> Yet, you're my favorite work of art.
>
> Is your figure less than Greek?
> Is your mouth a little weak?
> When you open it to speak, are you smart?
> But, don't change a hair for me.
> Not if you care for me.
> Stay little valentine, stay!
> Each day is Valentine's Day

---

[32] See Jean Vanier, *Befriending the Stranger,* pp. 59f.

[33] See *Aion,* CW 9ii, pars. 68ff.

Is your figure less than Greek?
Is your mouth a little weak?
When you open it to speak, are you smart?
But, don't change a hair for me.
Not if you care for me.
Stay little valentine, stay!
Each day is Valentine's Day.[34]

Of course it is not fair to enjoin your Valentine never to change. Everybody changes over time, and often for the better.

---

[34] Ella Fitzgerald, "My Funny Valentine," written by Lorenz Hart and Richard Rodgers; Lyrics © Warner/Chappell Music, Inc.

Time Top by Jerry Pethick (2001).

3
Badger Two
The Syzygy: Anima and Animus

Apparently Daemon is reluctant to repeat himself by expounding on this topic as he has often done, so I am obliged to take up the slack, as best I can, before proceeding with weighty matters. Well, why else am I here if not to be a back-up to my Master? Besides, without my help he would be twenty pages short of a book.

So here we go, first with an observation by Jung:

> The autonomy of the collective unconscious expresses itself in the figures of anima and animus. They personify those of its contents, which, when withdrawn from projection, can be integrated into consciousness. To this extent, both figures represent *functions* which filter the contents of the unconscious through to the conscious mind. . . . Though the effects of anima and animus can be made conscious, they themselves are factors transcending consciousness and beyond the reach of perception and volition. Hence they remain autonomous despite the integration of their contents, and for this reason they should be borne constantly in mind.[35]

Syzygy, what a strange name! What language is it? You won't find it in many English dictionaries. What could it mean, and why did Jung choose such an arcane term to describe the connection between the contrasexual archetypes?

Jung does not enlighten us in this essay with answers to such questions. But the late Edward F. Edinger, at the beginning of his masterful commentary on Jung's *Aion,* does:

> [Syzygy] means pair or couple. The pairs of aions that the Gnostic god emanated were called syzygies, but the original meaning of the word was "to yoke together." It is derived from two different stems: "syn" (Greek]

---

[35] "The Syzygy: Anima and Animus," *Aion,* CW 9ii, par. 40. (CW refers throughout to *The Collected Works of C.G. Jung.)*

meaning with, and "zygon" meaning yoke or the crossbar of a harness. The longitudinal bar of the harness is connected to the wagon as illustrated below and the cross bar is called the zygon. The necks of the horses slip into the two loops of the zygon. The zygon or the syzygy literally means the pair of horses that are yoked together in a single harness.[36]

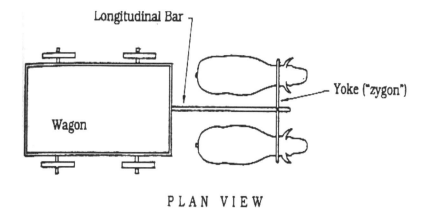

PLAN VIEW

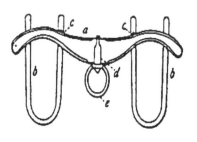

FRONT VIEW OF YOKE

Anima and animus, then, in Jung's formulation, are yoked together in the human psyche. What does this mean? It means they are fatefully conjoined, which as it happens may manifest in attraction or enmity.

---

[36] *The Aion Lectures: Exploring the Self in C. G. Jung's* Aion, p. 28.

What a novel concept to most moderns, the notion of a feminine personality in a man and a masculine figure in a woman's psyche. But it was gospel to the ancients, especially the Gnostics, a group of sects that flourished among the Greeks in the first few centuries A.D. They believed implicitly in the contrasexual nature of man and woman, which together produced Truth.

Before discussing the syzygy, Jung spends some pages delineating the lineaments of the shadow and the difficulties in apprehending it. He implies that the assimilation of the shadow is merely the apprentice-work, but integrating the anima or animus is the master-work.

Let us look closely at the two separately.

Jung had a number of descriptions and definitions of the anima, such as soul-image and "archetype of life itself,"[37] but in this essay he focuses on her as the "projection-making factor" in a man's psyche. She saves a man from being a stick-in-the-mud, prods him to adventure and the taking of risks, alternately enlivens and maddens him. And everything she does to him inside is reflected and amplified, through projection, in his activities and relationships in the outside world.

Psychologically the anima is both an archetype, a collective primordial image, and on the personal level a complex, functioning in a man as his soul. When a man is full of life he is "animated." The man with no connection to his inner woman feels dull and listless. Nowadays we call this depression, but the experience is not new. For thousands of years, among so-called primitive peoples, this state of being has been known as loss of soul.

A man's anima complex is initially determined by his experience of his personal mother or closest female caregiver. It is later modified through contact with other women—friends, lovers, relatives, teachers—but the experience of the personal mother is so powerful and long-lasting that a man is naturally attracted to those women who are much like her—or, as often happens, her direct opposite. That is to say, he may yearn for what he has known, or seek to escape it at all costs.

---

[37] "Archetypes of the Collective Unconscious," *The Archetypes and the Collective Unconscious,* CW 9I, par. 66.

A man who is unconscious of his feminine side is apt to see that aspect of himself, whatever its characteristics may be, in an actual woman. This happens via projection and is commonly experienced as falling in love, or, conversely, as intense dislike. Theoretically, falling in love (or hate) *means* that anima and animus have been constellated. A man may also project his anima onto another man, though in practice this is often difficult to distinguish from the projection of the man's shadow.

The man unrelated to his inner woman also tends to be moody, sometimes gentle and sentimental but prone to sudden rage and violence. Analysts call this being anima-possessed. By paying attention to his moods and emotional reactions—objectifying and personifying them—a man can come into possession of his soul rather than be possessed by it. As with any complex, the negative influence of the anima is reduced by establishing a conscious relationship with it.

Jung distinguished four broad stages of the anima in the course of a man's psychological development. He personified these, according to classical stages of eroticism, as Eve, Helen, Mary and Sophia.[38]

In the first stage, Eve, the man's anima is completely tied up with the mother—not necessarily his personal mother, but the image of woman as safe haven, faithful provider of nourishment, security and love. The man with an anima of this type cannot function well without a vital connection to a woman and is easy prey to being controlled by her. He frequently suffers impotence or has no sexual desire at all.

In the second stage, personified in the historical figure of Helen of Troy, the anima is a collective sexual image. She is Marlene Dietrich, Marilyn Monroe, Tina Turner, Madonna, all rolled up into one. The man under her spell is often a Don Juan who engages in repeated sexual adventures. These will invariably be short-lived, for two reasons: 1) he has a fickle heart—his feelings are whimsical and often gone in the morning—and 2) no real woman can live up to the expectations that go with this unconscious, ideal image.

---

[38] "The Psychology of the Transference," *The Practice of Psychotherapy,* CW 16, par. 361; see also Marie-Louise von Franz, "The Process of Individuation," in C. G. Jung, ed., *Man and His Symbols,* pp. 185f.

The third stage of the anima is Mary. It manifests in religious feelings and a capacity for genuine friendship with women. The man with an anima of this kind is able to see a woman as she is, independent of his own needs. His sexuality is integrated into his life, not an autonomous function that drives him. He can differentiate between love and lust. He is capable of lasting relationships because he can tell the difference between the object of his desire and his inner image of woman.

In the fourth stage, as Sophia (called Wisdom in the Bible), a man's anima functions as a guide to the inner life, mediating to consciousness the contents of the unconscious. Sophia is behind the need to grapple with the grand philosophical issues, the search for meaning. She is Beatrice in Dante's *Inferno,* and the creative muse in any artist's life. She is a natural mate for the archetypal "wise old man" in the male psyche. The sexuality of a man at this stage incorporates a spiritual or awesome dimension.

Theoretically, a man's anima development proceeds through these stages as he grows older and assimilates his experiences of the opposite sex. When the possibilities of one stage have been exhausted—which is to say, when adaptation to oneself and outer circumstances requires it—the psyche stimulates the move to the next stage.

In fact, the transition from one stage to another seldom happens without a struggle, for the psyche not only promotes and supports growth, it is also, paradoxically, conservative and loath to give up what it knows. Hence a psychological crisis is commonly precipitated when there is a pressing need for a man to move from one stage to the next.

For that matter, a man may have periodic contact with any number of anima images, at any time of life, depending on what is required to compensate the current dominant conscious attitude. The reality is that psychologically men live in a harem. Any man may observe this for himself by paying close attention to his dreams and fantasies. His soul-image appears in many different forms, as myriad as the expressions of an actual woman's femininity.

In subhuman guise, the anima may manifest as snake, toad, cat or bird; or on a slightly higher level as nixie, pixie, mermaid. In human form—to mention only a few personifications modeled on goddesses in Greek mythology—the anima may appear as Hera, consort and queen; Demeter/Persephone, the mother-daughter team; Aphrodite, the lover; Pallas Athene, carrier of culture and protectress of heroes; Artemis, the stand-offish huntress; and Hecate, ruler in the netherworld of magic.

The assimilation of a particular anima-image results in its death, so to speak. That is to say, as one personification of the anima is consciously understood, it is supplanted by another. Anima development in a man is thus a continuous process of death and rebirth. An overview of this process is very important in surviving the transition stage between one anima-image and the next. Just as no real woman relishes being discarded for another, so no anima-figure willingly takes second place to her upstart rival. In this regard, as in so much else involved in a person's psychological development, the good is the enemy of the better. To have contact with your inner woman at all is a blessing; to be tied to one that holds you back can be fatal.

While the old soul-mate clamors for the attention that now, in order for the man to move on, is demanded by and due to the new one, the man is often assailed by conflicting desires. The struggle is not just an inner, metaphorical one; it also involves his lived relationships with real women. The resultant suffering and inner turmoil, the tension and sleepless nights, are comparable to what occurs in any conflict situation.

The current anima-image that must be supplanted is often characterized in fairy tales as the false bride, while the new one is called the true bride. The essential difference between the two is captured in Marie-Louise von Franz's observation: "The truth of yesterday must be set aside for what is *now* the truth of one's psychic life."[39]

True and false brides don't come labeled, and so are difficult to recognize. A lot depends on a man's age, his position in life and how much work he has done on himself—particularly the extent to which he has already differentiated his soul-image from the other complexes teeming in his psyche.

Theoretically, there are two basic types of false bride. One is an anima

---

[39] *Redemption Motifs in Fairy Tales,* p. 85.

figure—or an actual woman—who leads a man into the fantasy realm, away from timely responsibilities in the outside world. The other is an inner voice—or again a real woman—that would tie a man to his persona when his real task is to turn inward, to find out what is behind the face he shows others.

The first type is commonly associated with the idealistic, and age-appropriate, attitudes of a younger man: the disinclination to compromise, a rigid response to the reality of everyday life. The second type of false bride is often associated with regressive tendencies in later life, evident in those who make feverish efforts to mask their age or reclaim their lost youth through younger companions, fitness regimes, face lifts, hair transplants and so on.

There is no hard and fast rule, however. An older man with too much unlived life may have to descend into the whore's cellar, so to speak, as part of his individuation process. The younger man with no ideals may be forced to develop some. Such things are the daily concerns of personal analysis.

As happens with any psychological content, the bride of either type, when not recognized as an inner reality, appears in the outside world through projection. If a man's anima is lonely and desperate for attention, he will tend to fall in love with dependent women who demand all his time and energy. The man with a mother-bound anima will get tied up with women who want to take care of him. The man not living up to his potential will fall for women who goad him on. In short, whatever qualities a man does not recognize in himself—shadow, anima, whatever—will confront him in real life. Outer reflects inner, that is the general rule. If there are any psychological rules that are valid always and everywhere, that is one of them.

The seductive lure of the false bride manifests in outer life not only as a tie to an unsuitable woman, but also as the wrong choice in a conflict situation. This is due to the regressive tendencies of the unconscious. Each new stage of development, each foothold on an increase in consciousness, must be wrested anew from the dragon-like grip of the past. This kind of work on oneself is called by Jung *contra naturam,* against nature. That is because nature is essentially conservative and unconscious. There is a lot to be said for the natural mind and the healthy instincts that go with it, but not much in terms of consciousness.

As the mediating function between the ego and the unconscious, the anima is complementary to the persona and stands in a compensatory relationship to it. That is to say, all those qualities absent from the outer attitude will be found in the inner. Jung gives the example of a tyrant tormented by bad dreams and gloomy forebodings:

> Outwardly ruthless, harsh, and unapproachable, he jumps inwardly at every shadow, is at the mercy of every mood, as though he were the feeblest and most impressionable of men. Thus his anima contains all those fallible human qualities his persona lacks.[40]

Similarly, when a man identifies with his persona, he is in effect possessed by the anima, with all the attendant symptoms. Jung:

> Identity . . . with the persona automatically leads to an unconscious identity with the anima because, when the ego is not differentiated from the persona, it can have no conscious relation to the unconscious processes. Consequently it *is* these processes, it is identical with them. Anyone who is himself his outward role will infallibly succumb to the inner processes; he will either frustrate his outward role by absolute inner necessity or else reduce it to absurdity, by a process of *enantiodromia.* He can no longer keep to his individual way, and his life runs into one deadlock after another. Moreover, the anima is inevitably projected upon a real object, with which he gets into a relation of almost total dependence.[41]

Thus it is essential for a man to distinguish between who he is and who he appears to be. Symptomatically, in fact, there is no significant difference between persona identification and anima possession; both are indications of unconsciousness.

Let us turn now to the animus.

A woman's inner image of men is strongly colored by her experience

---

[40] "Definitions," *Psychological Types,* CW 6, par. 804.

[41] Ibid., par. 807. *Enantiodromia* refers to the emergence of the unconscious opposite in the course of time.

of the personal father. Just as a man is apt to marry his mother, so to speak, so a woman is inclined to favor a man psychologically like her father; or, again, his opposite.

Whereas the anima in a man functions as his soul, a woman's animus is more like an unconscious mind. It manifests negatively in fixed ideas, unconscious assumptions and conventional opinions that may be generally right but just beside the point in a particular situation. A woman unconcious of her masculine side tends to be highly opinionated, critical and judgmental—animus-possessed. This kind of woman proverbially wears the pants; she rules the roost—or tries to. The men attracted to her may be driven to distraction by her whims, coldly emasculated, while she herself wears a mask of indifference to cover her insecurity.

A woman's animus becomes a helpful psychological factor only when she can tell the difference between "him" and herself. While a man's task in assimilating the anima involves discovering his true feelings, a woman must constantly question her collective ideas and opinions, measuring these against what *she* really thinks. If she does so, in time the animus can become a valuable inner companion who endows her with qualities of enterprise, courage, objectivity and spiritual wisdom.

Jung describes four stages of animus development in a woman, similar to those of the anima in a man. He first appears in dreams and fantasies as the embodiment of physical power, for instance an athlete or muscle man, a Samson or James Bond. This corresponds to the anima as Eve. For a woman with such an animus a man is simply a stud; he exists to give her physical satisfaction, protection and healthy babies.

In the second stage, analogous to the anima as Helen, the animus possesses initiative and the capacity for planned action. He is behind a woman's desire for independence and a career of her own. However, a woman with an animus of this type still relates to a man on a collective level: he is the generic husband-father, the man around the house whose primary role is to provide shelter and support for his family—Mr. Do-All, Mr. Fix-It, with no life of his own.

In the next stage, corresponding to the anima as Mary, the animus is the Word, often personified in dreams as a professor, clergyman or some other authoritarian figure. A woman with such an animus has a great respect for traditional learning; she is capable of sustained creative work and welcomes the opportunity to exercise her mind. She is able to relate to a man on an individual level, as friend or lover rather than husband or father, and she ponders her own elusive identity.

In the fourth stage, the animus is the incarnation of spiritual meaning—a Mahatma Gandhi, Martin Luther King Jr. or Dalai Lama. On this highest level, like the anima as Sophia, the animus mediates between a woman's conscious mind and the unconscious. In mythology he appears as Hermes, messenger of the gods, or Iris, goddess of the rainbow, connecting heaven and earth; in dreams he is a helpful guide. Sexuality for such a woman is imbued with spiritual significance.

Any of these aspects of the animus can be projected onto a man, who will be expected to live up to the projected image—or else. As mentioned earlier, the same is true of the anima. So in any relationship between a man and a woman there are at least four personalities involved, as shown in the diagram (next page).[42]

The most positive aspects of a woman's animus manifest when she has assimilated it, consciously integrated it. Jung writes:

> Just as the anima becomes, through integration, the Eros of consciousness, so the animus becomes a Logos; and in the same way that the anima gives relationship and relatedness to a man's consciousness, the animus gives to woman's consciousness a capacity for reflection, deliberation, and self-knowledge.[43]

Theoretically, there is no difference between an unconscious man and a woman's tyrannical animus. The implication is that an unconscious man can be coerced into being or doing whatever a woman wants. But it's just as true the other way around: unconscious women are easily seduced by a man's anima. In relationships there are no innocent victims.

---

[42] Adapted from Jung's drawing in "The Psychology of the Transference," *The Practice of Psychotherapy,* CW 16, par. 422.

[43] "The Syzygy: Anima and Animus," *Aion,* CW 9ii, par. 33.

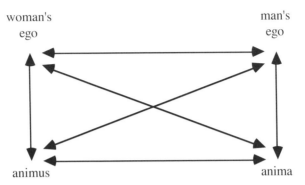

woman's ego   man's ego

animus   anima

The more differentiated a woman is in her own femininity, the more able she is to reject whatever unsuitable role is projected onto her by a man. This forces the man back on himself. If he has the capacity for self-examination and insight, he may discover in himself the basis for false expectations. Failing inner resources on either side, there is only rancor and animosity; e.g., Thursday colliding with Friday.

Analogous to the true and false anima-brides discussed above, there are true and false bridegrooms. The latter may manifest as a woman's feelings of worthlessness and despair, and in her outer life as a compulsive tie to, say, an authoritarian father figure or an abusive partner. The true bridegroom gives her confidence in herself, encourages her endeavors and is interested in her mind as well as her body.

In the best of all possible worlds, the true bridegroom finds his mate in the true bride, and vice versa. Of course, this is no guarantee that they will live happily ever after. No matter how individuated one is, no matter how much one has worked on oneself, projection and conflict in relationships are always possible, if not inevitable. But that is no bad thing; we are human, after all, and such things keep us on our toes.

Intimate relationships are fraught with difficulty. There are any number of landmines to be negotiated before two people feel comfortable with each other; more when they become sexually involved, and more again if and when they live together. On top of projection and identification, there are each other's personal complexes and typological differences. In truth, the very things that brought them together in the first place are just as likely to drive them apart.

Assuming that most relationships begin with mutual good will, why do so many end in acrimony? There are probably as many answers to this as there are couples who split up, but in terms of a common pattern, typology certainly plays a major role, as outlined in an earlier chapter in the *Jung Uncorked* series.[44]

The yoking together of anima and animus is almost always full of animosity, which is to say, loaded with emotion. Jung puts it quite graphically:

> When animus and anima meet, the animus draws his sword of power and the anima ejects her poison of illusion and seduction.[45]

How, then, is one to work on a relationship? Now, I am no expert, having burned as many bridges as I have built, but I have some suggestions.

You work on a relationship by shutting your mouth when you are ready to explode; by not inflicting your affect on the other person; by quietly leaving the battlefield and tearing your hair out; by asking yourself—not your partner—what complex in you was activated, and to what end. The proper question is not, "Why is she doing that to me?" or "Who does he think he is?" but rather, "Why am I reacting in this way?—Who do *I* think he or she is?" And more: "What does this say about my psychology? What can I do about it?" Instead of accusing the other person of driving you crazy, you say to yourself, "I feel I'm being driven crazy—where, or who, in me is that coming from?" It also helps to personify the animus or anima; give him or her a name and have a dialogue with that person. In this way you bring it all home, where it belongs.

That is how, over time, you establish a container, a personal temenos, a safe haven independent of your mate or anyone else.

It is true that a strong emotion sometimes needs to be expressed, because it comes not from a complex but from genuine feeling. There is a fine line between the two, and it is extremely difficult to tell one from the other without a container. But when you can tell the difference you can

---

[44] See Sharp, *Jung Uncorked,* Book One, chap. 6, "The Type Problem" and chap. 7, "The Problem of the Attitude-Type."

[45] "The Syzygy: Anima and Animus," *Aion,* CW 9ii, par. 30.

speak from the heart.

Working on a relationship involves keeping your mood to yourself and examining it. You neither bottle up the emotion nor allow it to poison the air. The merit in this approach is that it throws us back entirely on our experience of ourselves. It is foolish to imagine we can change the person who seems to be the cause of our heartache. But with the proper container we can change ourselves and our reactions.

It used to be thought that "letting it all hang out" was the thing to do. But that is merely allowing the complex to take over. The trick is to get some distance from the complex, objectify it, take a stand toward it. You can't do this if you identify with it, if you can't tell the difference between yourself and the emotion that grabs you by the throat when a complex is active. And you can't do it without a container.

Those who think that talking about a relationship will help it get better put the cart before the horse. Work on yourself and a good relationship will follow. You can either accept who you are and find a relationship that fits, or twist yourself out of shape and get what you deserve.

The endless blather that takes place between two complexed people solves nothing. It is a waste of time and energy and as often as not actually makes the situation worse. It is worth saying again:

> When animus and anima meet, the animus draws his sword of power and the anima ejects her poison of illusion and seduction.[46]

Of course, the meeting between anima and animus is not always negative. In the beginning, at least, the two are just as likely to be starry-eyed lovers. Later, when reality sets in and the bloom is off the rose, they may even become fast friends. But the major battles in close relationships occur because the man has not withdrawn his anima projection on the woman, and/or the woman still projects her animus onto the man.

We may understand this intellectually, but when someone we love does not behave according to the image we have of him or her, all hell breaks loose. We are instantly complexed. Our emotions do not coincide with what is in our heads or hearts. Our reactions run the gamut between

---

[46] Ibid.

outright violence, seething anger, self-righteousness and grieved silence, depending on our psychology. Whatever the immediate reaction, it is bound to happen again unless we reflect on what is behind it.

I give you George, successful advertising executive in his mid-forties, happily married with three grown sons. He came to see Daemon because he was obsessed with a young woman he barely knew. In our third session together he showed me a letter he had written her:

Dear Ms. Cotton Pants,

It is close to midnight, an ungodly hour to exorcise demons, but I have to declare myself. I have torn myself away from Hitchcock movies on the television to tell you that I am besotted with you.

You may not remember me. Well, that's no surprise. You wouldn't notice me in a crowd, and we only brushed shoulders once at a concert hall some months ago. I saw the moon in your eyes and I was immediately smitten, don't ask me why. I tracked you down and I have stalked you ever since. Oh, don't be afraid, I mean you no harm.

Now, I don't wish to be importunate, but I must see you in order to stay sane. Perhaps we can meet some day for coffee and a bagel. Please say yes, it would mean so much to me. I can be reached at Butterfield 9062, any time of day or night. Just ask for George. Please help!

"I haven't sent it," said George, tearfully. "I wanted to talk to you first." He showed me a picture of a cute seventeen-year-old.

I cannot divulge details of our subsequent conversations, but I can say that George was relieved to hear that his plight was not unique and that he was not certifiably crazy. He gladly absorbed what I told him about the phenomenon of projection and he was open to the possibility of a feminine side of himself that he saw in "Ms. Cotton Pants," a fanciful moniker he associated with a teenage girlfriend, a cheerleader who brazenly flashed her undies in public but locked knees in private. He also confessed that when watching movies he often imagined her in the role of the heroine. Well, it was not long before George stopped obsessing about Ms. Cotton Pants and turned his attention to his wife.

Jung ends his brief essay on the syzygy by emphasizing the disruptive power of anima and animus as long as they remain unconscious and projected:

Those who do not see them are in their hands, just as a typhus epidemic flourishes best when its source is undiscovered. . . . What we can discover about them from the conscious side is so slight as to be almost imperceptible. It is only when we throw light into the dark depths of the psyche and explore the strange and tortured paths of human fate that it gradually becomes clear to us how immense is the influence wielded by these two factors that complement our conscious life.[47]

Consider this: zoologists have observed that among a certain breed of fish, the *cichlidae,* a male can combine sex with aggression, but not sex and fear. In the female, sex and fear can be combined, but not aggression and sex. Jung's analyst-colleague Marie-Louise von Franz sees this little-known fact as a psychological verity applicable to the behavior of humans, stating, "There you have the animus-anima problem in a nutshell."[48] Now, this sounds like an outlandish proposition, for it implies that a woman may mate with a man she is afraid of, but a man is rendered impotent by an aggressive woman.

Well, I wouldn't know about that. All I know for sure is that in the best of loving circumstances there is a satisfying congruence between giving oneself and being taken.

****

Now if I dare to make a direct statement about Jung's essential message, it is that *the purpose of human life is to become conscious.* In a 1927 lecture Jung writes: "The reason why consciousness exists, and why there is an urge to widen and deepen it, is very simple: without consciousness, things go less well" Just think on that for a while—without consciousness things go less well"[49]—and see where it takes you. Put it beside Jung's belief that the unexamined life is not worth living, and it seems to me that you have both Jung's motivation for all his work and the primary reason for the ever-growing collective interest in it.

---

[47] Ibid., par. 41.

[48] Von Franz, *The Problem of the Puer Aeternus,* p. 173.

[49] "Analytical Psychology and *Weltanschauung,"* *The Structure and Dynamics of the Psyche* CW 8, par. 695.

Jung defined consciousness as the function or activity that maintains the relation of psychic contents to the ego; in that way he distinguished it conceptually from the *psyche,* which is made up of both consciousness and the unconscious. And so, in Jung's model, the ego is not identical with consciousness, it is simply the central complex of the conscious mind Jung also believed that there is no consciousness without the discrimination of opposites. Now, the primary opposites are ego-consciousness and the unconscious, but in fact becoming conscious involves discriminating between a whole range of opposites, of which masculine and feminine, and good and evil, are only two.

Jung described two distinct ways in which consciousness arises. One is during a moment of high emotional tension involving a situation in the outer world, which Jung compared to the scene in Parsifal (in the Grail legend) where the hero, at the very moment of greatest temptation, suddenly realizes the meaning of the Fisher King's wound. The other happens in a state of contemplation where ideas pass before the mind like dream-images. Then suddenly there is a flash of association between two apparently disconnected and widely separated ideas. We commonly experience such things as revelations.

In Jung's model of the psyche, consciousness is a superstructure based on, and arising out of, the unconscious. Here is how he describes it:

> Consciousness does not create itself—it wells up from unknown depths. In childhood it wakes each morning out of the depths of sleep from an unconscious condition. It is like a child that is born daily out of the primordial womb of the unconscious. . . . It is not only influenced by the unconscious but continually emerges out of it in the form of numberless spontaneous ideas and sudden flashes of thought.[50]

Overall, Jung believed that consciousness is dependent on a working relationship between a strong but flexible ego and the Self, regulating center of the psyche. This relationship is part and parcel of what Jung called individuation. Becoming conscious involves waking up to why we do what we do, by becoming aware of the many ways we are influenced

---

[50] "The Psychology of Eastern Meditation," *Psychology and Religion,* CW 11, par. 935.

by unconscious aspects of ourselves (e.g. complexes). But Jung left us with a body of knowledge and a number of tools useful in narrowing the gap between ego and the unconscious. In very practical terms, he showed how our personal psychology affects our interactions with other people.

Take opinions, for instance. Opinions are as common as potatoes. Everyone has his or her own collection of potatoes, and some of them are very hot. Where do opinions come from? According to Jungian theory, behind opinions there are feeling-toned complexes, and as long as we are unconscious of how they affect what we believe and say and do, we are at their mercy. We may even confuse our personal opinions with objective truth. I believe such and such, therefore it must be true, and anyone who doesn't agree is either stupid or perverse. What is more, we tend to identify with our opinions and to feel threatened by those who don't share them. On a collective level this has arguably been the stimulus for many wars. Closer to home, it can destroy relationships.

About seventy years ago the American humorist James Thurber wrote a short story called "The Breaking Up of the;." It's about a married couple, Gordon and Marcia Winship. She declares that Greta Garbo is the greatest actor in the world while he insists that Donald Duck is. It escalates and escalates until finally they divorce. It's a delightful little sketch and a good illustration of the acrimony and craziness that regularly results when one is possessed by a complex.

How To Identify an Alien

Listen up now. A human man or woman cannot without acrobatic prowess put their both feet into trousers (or slacks) at the same time. Aliens can. I have seen it done. So, be alert. If you catch your mate shoving their two feet into pants at the same time (including shorts, underwear and skirts), your mate may be someone from another world. Now, this does not mean you should love him or her any the less. Just be wary, for some aliens are not assimilated to Earthly ways, which can give rise to petty squabbles (e.g., Thursday colliding with Friday), and even if your mate is not an alien, it is a good reminder that everyone has a shadow and a contrasexual complex.

Well, the above may not actually be true, but as I said to El Jay, "That doesn't matter; I wrote it and that's true enough for me"; also, a little levity never hurt anyone.

Jennifer Morgan, star of the Broadway hit, "I am a Daisy."

4
Daemon Two
My Undiscovered Self

Just as man, as a social being, cannot in the long run exist without a tie to the community, so the individual will never find the real justification for his existence and his own spiritual and moral autonomy anywhere except in an extramundane principle capable of relativizing the overpowering influence of external factors. The individual who is not anchored in God can offer no resistance on his own resources to the physical and moral blandishments of the world. For this he needs the evidence of inner, transcendent experience which alone can protect him from the otherwise inevitable submersion in the mass.[51]

Deep suffering makes noble. It separates [individual from collective].
—Friedrich Nietzsche.

I have been told that I am a remarkable individual. I like that. I don't have a swole head about it, but nothing remarkable comes about without a degree of pain and suffering along the way. We all have a remarkable journey. I write about mine.

I am often overwhelmed by my self-imposed tasks. Take this book, for instance. No one is waiting for what I have to say. But I continue to grapple with it, ponder and lose sleep, feel inadequate. However, as they say, it goes with the territory.

"The Undiscovered Self" was actually my first acquaintance with Jung. It was 1960. I was a very young man, a self-important "struggling writer" in London, England, when I came across it, a slim paperback edition, on a used book stall on a London bridge. I bought it on impulse for one shilling. Now, some fifty years later, I am at pains to recall its initial

---

[51] "The Undiscovered Self," *Civilization in Transition,* CW 10, par. 511.

impact, which as a matter of fact did not bear any noticeable fruit in my life until many years later. But perhaps that is precisely why I have chosen to comment on this essay from the many others in Jung's *Collected Works*—to conjure up the excitement and enthusiasm I felt when I first read it.

Psychologically naïve, I could not for ages fathom the difference between lower-case self and capital Self. But the very title implied that I didn't know myself, however spelled, and perhaps that is what hooked me—my own ignorance.

In those long-ago days, I was still attached to the collective by an umbilical cord about two thousand miles long. I had left Procter & Gamble (and a 1956 Ford Thunderbird convertible) for a fantasy life in Europe, and I was going nowhere but down. In time I fell helplessly in love, convinced my sweetheart to marry and we had a child, then another and another. I think I was a decent father, but being a "momma's boy" I was a quintessential *puer* and not much good at being a husband.[52] I know this only in retrospect, for I was extraverted at the time and not much given to introspection.

So, I had left the corporate world behind, spurred on by such mid-century anti-establishment classics as William Whyte's *The Organization Man* and Philip Wylie's wildly acerbic *Generation of Vipers* with its passionate polemic against "Momism." However, I suffered greatly from the loss of community and a value system I had grown up with and heartily embraced for a couple of years as an up-and-coming, bushy-tailed young executive—values based on materialism, ambition, upper-mobility, success, etc.; everything we loosely call, even in Canada, "the American way of life." I had rebelled *against,* but I wasn't *for* anything but myself—individualism of the most egregious kind.[53] I had no interest

---

[52] For the definitive study of this syndrome, see Marie-Louise von Franz, *The Problem of the Puer Aeternus.* Presumedly, the puer/senex dyad is latent throughout life, and the energies of one or other manifest when appropriate to compensate our ego-conscious imbalance. See also Ann Yeoman, *Now or Neverland: Peter Pan and the Myth of Eternal Youth.*

[53] Curiously, the words "individualism" and "individuation" do not appear in this essay. The difference, to be very brief, is that the former bespeaks a "me first" outsider attitude,

in politics or religion, or any other "ism," and without a new foundation to replace the old order, I hovered in mid-air, rootless. I was as ripe for cult-conversion as any country hick just off the bus in New York. Gnu knows how I escaped that, or even if I did.

I wrote and wrote, but the world did not welcome my turgid tomes, and rightly so, for I had little inside me worth writing about. I acted like a clever fellow, and even believed I was as I pecked away on my portable Smith-Corona in a hut at the foot of the garden, but I felt like the Beatles' nowhere man, making all his nowhere plans for nobody— "doesn't have a point of view, knows not where he's going to. . . ."

I had left my well-paid junior-executive, public relations job at P & G simply because I found it "meaningless"—though I was fuzzy as to what that meant (except for the banality of the products I was obliged to promote), and for a long time I found nothing to replace it. I was floating, bereft.

In Europe, falling among literary friends, I was soon seduced by, and found temporary solace in, such iconic writers as Kafka, Kierkegaard, Nietzsche, Rilke, Dostoyevsky, Camus, Henry Miller, Samuel Beckett and a dozen others of that ilk. Their work excited me no end, but the best I could do was mimic them. They buoyed me for a time; I could read a line and write four pages, but their outlook on life was essentially negative and ultimately too bleak (except of course for Henry Miller's bawdy novels) to sustain the fun-loving WASP I was, flirtatiously haunting Chelsea pubs, hitchhiking around Europe, or making out with English lovelies during coffee-breaks on the roof deck of Harrod's department store, where I worked for a time packing books. It was the age of so-called free love, after all, though in the long run I and some others of my generation paid a pretty psychic penny for our cavalier attitude toward Eros. Not that I regret an ounce of those premarital sown oats, not on your nelly. That would be forsaking my essentially middle-class roots and my first-grown-up lover, a spirited colleen from Winnipeg who liked

---

while individuation is a process of becoming who you were meant to be, within and related to a collective. (See my *Jung Lexicon: A Primer of Terms & Concepts* for fuller descriptions.)

dancing and me loving her from behind. I was truly reluctant to leave her, and cried as I sailed off on a freighter to my problematic future in Europe.

Into this void of a personality dropped C. G. Jung and "The Undiscovered Self" for the princely sum of one shilling (about U.S. 25 cents then), which incidentally was the average hourly wage of an English manual laborer in the early 1960s. I know this bit of trivia because I dug ditches between stints of teaching in those horrid British secondary-modern schools, where half the kids were hooligans and the other half asleep. (Another chapter in my never-to-be novel.)[54]

Well, I finally became bored eating my heart out in that hut, and in the mid-sixties talked my way into a graduate program at the newly-founded University of Sussex in Brighton. It involved literature and philosophy under the umbrella title of "The Modern European Mind," just my meat. This resulted in a masters thesis entitled "In Search of the Self," an immodestly ambitious comparative study of the work of D. H. Lawrence, Soren Kierkegaard and Jean-Jacques Rousseau. Here is a brief excerpt from the introduction:

> Rousseau, Kierkegaard, Lawrence. These figures are apparently as diverse as could be: Rousseau, eighteenth-century French paranoic; Kierkegaard, nineteenth-century Danish religious introvert; Lawrence, twentieth-century English inconoclast. Yet they have at least this much in common: their work reflects a concern for the individual and his or her development, Each, in his own original way, explores the implications of his belief in the nature of the self.

Now, if I had been more widely read in Jung's work, I would have included him in my thesis under the rubric "The Psychological Self," for as I now know, in Jung's work the "search for the self" assumes a depth dimension that in the other three is either blurred or not present at all. This is because Jung makes a fundamental distinction between the mundane ego-self and the Self as center of the psyche, or, in his language, the

---

[54] Frank McCourt has chronicled better than I ever could this frustrating experience, albeit in the New York school system, in his novels *'Tis* and *Teacher Man.*

"archetype of wholeness." Beside Jung, the others fall far short; their limitations are a result of not discriminating between ego-consciousness and the unconscious.

Indeed, my thesis might as well have been called "In Search of Meaning," for that was what I was really after. And in Jung's thought-provoking essay I found it, in spades. Without a bye your leave, and hardly noticing it, from an existentialist I became an essentialist.[55]

The passage that heads this chapter is the one that struck me most forcefully on initial reading. *Extramundane principle! Transcendent experience!* Wow. These were new concepts to me. I had written about "echoing depths," but I was talking through my hat—I didn't really have a clue what I meant by that.

But as I became more steeped in Jung, I realized that the writers I most admired were involved in mining their own unconscious. And in fact, it was a sense of the transcendent (a new word to me) that was notably absent from my irreligious upbringing (limited to story-telling at United Church Sunday School and bingo in church basements with my gramma). And transcendent!—something of, but at the same time outside of, myself to believe in and to experience; something beyond the daily grind, something other-worldly, even irrational. I might have found this in other ways or other writers if I had known what to look for, but I didn't, and only serendipitously chanced upon it in Jung's celebration of the individual, real man as opposed to the corporate, statistical man I had been conditioned by my culture to become.

I have since realized how difficult it is for anyone to escape the influence of the environment they grow up in. I think "brain-washing" is not too strong a term for what we are inculcated to expect and want as adults. It is an unconscious endeavor in tune with the culture.

In my early working life, being the editor of P & G's in-house magazine *Moonbeams* was fun and interesting and moreover conferred a persona-status I enjoyed and found hard to do without. I was twenty-one

---

[55] I am indebted to Jungian analyst J. Gary Sparks for this concise distinction: "The existentialist says we create ourselves. The essentialist says we discover ourselves." *(At the Heart of Matter: Synchronicity and Jung's Spiritual Testament, pp. 125f.)*

years old. My only previous work experience was a summer job as a SHORAN (SHort Range Aerial Navigation) ground operator at an Eskimo base on Coral Island in the middle of Hudson's Bay, receiving radio signals from airplanes mapping the north. Then suddenly, straight out of university with a journalism degree, I was recruited by P & G to be the Director of Public Relations for Canada. They flew me to head office in Cincinnati and gave me a Leica camera. I was captain of the company bowling team. I had stock options, benefits and a pension plan, a secure future. I had a midnight blue suit and a key to the executive washroom! I was starting at the top. Now I ask you, talk about inflation. For some months, I was cock of the walk among the pretty secretaries.

When I forsook that job, my father, who had worked his way up through the ranks of the RCAF (Royal Canadian Air Force) to become an officer, said sadly, "Son, you'll always regret it." And for some months I did. In London, between excitements at the opera, ballet and in pubs, I was homesick and thought of going back to resume my "proper place" in my culture, my society. It was my first *crise de foie* (crisis of faith).

"Struggling writer" just didn't cut it—harder work and few outer rewards. I didn't know then that as a Capricorn I was fated by the stars (or say the gods, why not) to reap a harvest later in life.[56] However, I continued to practice my craft and eventually persuaded London publishers to pay me for editing manuscripts and compiling indexes, a tedious and exacting task I had never done before.

In "The Undiscovered Self," writing at the height of the Cold War, Jung offers no easy solutions to the contemporary crisis in world affairs. Instead he declares that the alternative to world annihilation depends not upon mass movements for good or on idealistic appeals to reason, but rather upon a recognition of the existence of good and evil in every individual and a true understanding of the secular soul. "The Undiscovered Self" is, as the *New York Times Book Review* noted at the time, a "passionate plea for individual integrity."[57]

---

[56] As it happens, my astrological birth-mates include Richard Nixon and Marie-Louise von Franz. It's what you call a mixed blessing.

[57] Back cover, Mentor edition, 1958.

Well, I was a complete novice in the field of psychology. My studies in mathematics and physics had left little room for the humanities. I knew nothing of Freud's ubiquitous influence in the modern world. Shoot! I had hardly even heard of the sub- or unconscious except as a garbage bin of repressed wishes to sleep with one parent or the other. I was not an intellectual, that's for sure, but I prided myself on being a scientist and a reasonable "child of the Enlightenment." Logos prevailed in my world; sex too, but how was a young fella to learn of Eros?

Imagine, even at the time I abandoned physics for journalism, Ernest Hemingway's laconic style, more or less bereft of adjectives and adverbs, was the model for "clean prose," called objectivity when I worked for the Canadian Press news agency: who, what, why, where and when, but little feeling except maybe, if you were intuitive, between the lines.

North America in the mid-twentieth century was a macho, patriarchal world where the feminine in general was of little account outside the kitchen and the bedroom—but only on the surface, while underneath, behind the curtains, women held the reins of power as they always have since time immemorial on account of their magically inspiriting yoni. Feminists may roll their eyes, but that's the way it is. I did not make this up in my head. Most men are just large children, easy prey to their instincts and more or less in constant need of mothering.[58]

Anyway, all in all, Jung's essay was for me a wake-up call, an epiphany of sorts, for its essential message was that the visible, everyday world is not all there is, and that the hidden side of ourselves, the unconscious, of which we know very little, has a greater say in our attitudes and behavior patterns than most of us realize. It is true that Freud was there first, though not *the* first,[59] and certainly not for me.

I think "The Undiscovered Self" speaks especially to those who have lost, or never had, a religious or creedal belief. Jung acknowledges that organized religion, of whatever stripe, has traditionally been a counter-

---

[58] The best book I know on this syndrome is Marie-Louise Von Franz, *The Problem of the Puer Aeternus.*

[59] See Henri F. Ellenberger, *The Discovery of the Unconscious.*

balance to mass-mindedness as well as the middleman, so to speak, between a Higher Power and our mundane concerns. Nor does he dispute the fact that Church dogma, whatever atrocities it may have been responsible for over the ages (e.g., the Inquisition), has been the saving factor in many an individual life. But Jung distinguishes a creed from a religion:

> A creed gives expression to a definite collective belief, whereas the word *religion* [from Latin *religere,* meaning the careful observation and consideration of irrational factors] expresses a subjective relationship to certain metaphysical, extramundane factors. A creed is a confession of faith intended chiefly for the world at large and is thus an intramundane affair, while the meaning and purpose of religion lie in the relationship of the individual to God (Christianity, Judaism, Islam) or to the path of salvation and liberation (Buddhism). From this basic fact all ethics is derived, which without the individual's responsibility before God can be called nothing more than conventional morality.
>
> . . . A creed coincides with the established Church or, at any rate, forms a public institution whose members include not only true believers but vast numbers of people who can only be described as "indifferent" in matters of religion and who belong to it simply by force of habit. Here the difference between a creed and a religion becomes palpable. [60]

Elsewhere Jung describes religion in terms of a certain attitude of mind—"the attitude peculiar to a consciousness which has been changed by experience of the numinosum"—the awesome or holy unknown. [61] By all accounts, such experience is rather rare since the Middle Ages, and consequently the equivalent of religious authority is relegated by default to the State. Jung writes:

> The policy of the State is exalted to a creed, the leader or party boss becomes a demigod beyond good and evil, and his votaries are honoured as heroes, martyrs, apostles, missionaries. There is only *one* truth... It is sacrosanct and above criticism. Anyone who thinks differently is a heretic, who, as we know from history, is threatened with all manner of unpleasant things. [62]

---

[60] "The Undiscovered Self," *Civilization in Transition,* CW 10, pars. 507f.

[61] "Psychology and Religion," *Psychology and Religion,* CW 11, par. 9.

[62] "The Undiscovered Self," *Civilization in Transition,* CW 10, par. 511.

That passage obviously refers to dictatorships, but it is arguably applicable in democracies too. The recent U.S. presidential Bush years come to mind, as does President Dwight D. Eisenhower's warning in the 1950s about the military-industrial "complex," though Ike might not have realized that his words had psychological overtones.

Well, there are many other cogent passages I could quote here, for it is a long essay, about fifty pages; but I think I have given you the gist of its overall import, which is that when the collective rules, individuality will inevitably be driven to the wall. I have little more to say about it, except that it prepared me, well in advance, to accept my improbable evolution from a physicist into a Jungian analyst and publisher of books by other analysts. A life with meaning was Jung's unwitting gift to me, and "The Undiscovered Self" was my first intimation of it.

And by the way, in a subtle twist of the pickled finger of fate, the house I now live and work in is just around the corner from the office I used to have at Procter & Gamble. Synchronicity, anyone?

Well, that was almost sixty years ago. I think that if I had stayed with P & G I would now be either head of the company or dead. Either way I'd be in Hell, where I may be anyway, but at least on my own terms.

No wonder older men seek younger women to love. I keep hearing or reading about older women near my age still interested in sex, but I haven't met any. On occasion I have proposed romance to some, and been met with disdainful remarks to put me off (e.g., had enough of "that stuff"), or counterproposals of friendship, which is enough to drop them off my radar—except for one, my friend Rebecca, to whom I am entirely and chastely devoted.

I do love women, after all, but I know when I'm not wanted (and there's no point in flogging a dead horse, as the saying goes). Now, to want and be wanted and not act on it, that is something to be treasured in my old kit bag, where my loverNot Rebecca nestles unchallenged.

Okay, I can get foolish late at night or early in the morning but what else is one to do without a mate to play cribbage or frolic with? I listen to jazz and write to fill the gap between my fantasies and reality.

In any case, a woman's desire is difficult to gauge, for it comes and goes like the phases of the moon. This consternates men, who generally can make love at the drop of a panty-hose. These biological realities often collide with disturbing results (e.g., quarrels, divorce, murder even).

So you can betcha—if I'm not eating or making love, I am writing. That is how a shadow-complex plays out in everyday life. For some people it's sex on the run, for others it may be gambling, cooking, caffeine or climbing a bunch of mountains; for me it's writing. Of course I have a sex complex too, but who doesn't? That is evolutionary psychology 101.[63]

I may well die from emphysema (as did my mother), but that is just a blanket term for CHF (congestive heart failure), which anyone who survives cancer eventually dies from anyway. I mean, the doctors really don't know much more than that, like my specialist said to me about my hurting feet: "You have peripheral neuropathy. We don't know exactly what that means and we can't cure it, but we can treat it." Welcome to ideopathy versus iatrogenisis.

I thanked him and walked away with a prescription for Gabapentin. I don't like pharmaceuticals on principle, but I've been taking these for three years, and they do help relieve my poor feet.

I guess the bottom line is that doctors are as baffled as anyone else about the aging process. They can echo Dr. Seuss's ironic advice, "You're only old once"[64]—but otherwise hold your hand and wish you luck.

****

Yesterday my friend Cynthia dropped in to read the Bhagavad-Gita together. She's a smart lady, inclined to Buddhist teachings, past and future lives, that kind of thing. Such esoterica did not really interest me, but her body did. I might note here that since as a teenager I realized that beneath a female's fur there was a hidden treasure, I have been interested in mining the feminine, body and soul. It is fair to say I had, and still have, a labia fetish (i.e., complex); I call it a search for Eros. Well, that's my

---

[63] See Anthony Stevens, *The talking Cure, Book Three.*

[64] See Dr. Seuss, "You're Only Old Once; A Book For Obsolete Children,"

post-doc research project.

We went over a few pages, and then Cynthia faded.

"Oh, I'm so tired," she said.

I led her upstairs to my bed and laid her gently down.

I lay beside and touched her cheek. I was overwhelmed with the desire to please her; that's the way I am.

"I want to lick you all over," I suddenly said.

"Well, help yourself and do adore me," she replied with a little wiggle, shucking her frock.

Now, I did a lot of licking and Cynthia was positively ready to go. I was more than keen to consummate our tryst, but as sometimes happens to elderly badgers, I was limper than a dead fish. Disappointing, no big deal for me, but for Cynthia? I wanted her not to feel at fault.

"Sweetheart," I said, "It's my problem."

Cynthia picked up her books and blew me a kiss as she left.

"Try Viagra," she threw back at me over her shoulder.

After Cynthia left, I got to thinking about what had happened. Well, I am reflective by nature. It's not the first time I couldn't manage to couple with a desirable lady. I have to ask myself, is it physical or psychological? Is it the heart bypass? The lack of exercise? My generally poor circulation? This is an ongoing riddle for me to wrestle with whenever it happens, and I don't take it lightly.

In the deep of the night, it is natural to long for a mate, while forgetting the consequences of having one—the petty cuts, the mutual complexes. One focuses on someone to give and receive love. That is natural in the deep of the night, whether you're a badger or a daemon.

Well, that's enough of dystopia, what might have been, what might be. Now let's dive into the heart of the beast.

> Deep suffering makes noble. It separates [individual from collective].
> —Nietzsche.

When I'm not eating or making love, I am writing. Trust me. Of course, I may do the laundry or the dishes along the way, but my brain is still shuffling words. And once in a while I venture out for groceries; after all,

I am not homeless and I don't live under a bridge. When I am staring at the wall, or walking, my thoughts are rumbling and I am writing, writing, writing. By the time I am satisfied with a manuscript, there is not a sentence or a paragraph that I haven't rewritten at least a dozen times, or even a hundred. That is what writing a book is all about—editing your original, raw material until you're almost sick of it; but you persevere because you have something to say—or nothing else to do.

Anyway, after writing, my next greatest love is women in all their grandeur—exposed or undercover—the feminine mystique. There is a term for this common addiction. It is called being a man (but you won't find it in the psychiatrist's DSM (Diagnostic and Statistical Manual). Of course, women have something to do with this too, as they willingly or unconsciously accept a man's projections onto them for motives of their own. But I won't go there just now.

My teenage sweetheart Deedee and I fooled around a lot, but my first attempt to fornicate was not with her but with a sweet young dance partner in my father's 1948 fluid-drive De Soto. She too was a virgin and we fumbled in vain to fit our parts together. I think her name was Nancy. The next day I sailed to France, where I found a willing teacher in the art of love, and incidentally my vocation as a writer. By the time I returned to visit Nancy, I was married and so was she. I was morally flexible, but Nancy was firmly Catholic and loyal to her wedding vows. Bad on me for being a jerk.

****

I let Badger McGee get away with a lot in this book, because on the whole I think he is right that Western civilization, if not the whole world, is going to Hell in a handbasket—thanks to climate change and the lack of pollen for bees that survive colony collapse disorder (CCD); and remember that we humans depend on bees to pollinate about 90% of what we eat! I did not make this up in my head; it is a true fact.

I think Badger has an appropriate attitude toward current reality. He is a small, underground creature. He leaves quite a little carbon footprint in the grand scheme of things. He burrows, he reflects, and willy-nilly he records his aberrant thoughts. He has considered going into politics, just because Toronto City Hall is a disaster these days. But Badger is much too introverted to venture into the public sphere. He is not ambitious; he eschews suits; he has some distasteful habits, and he does not seek supremacy over nature. Indeed, Badger and his like may very well outlive the human race as we know it—greedy, arrogant, belligerent, and inflated with power.

Now, early in the twenty-first century, we are all inheritors, dare I say victims, of the Renaissance, a predominantly rational view of life (let's call it Logos, why not) that left behind all the gods, demons and angels, the mysteries, that surrounded mankind for several previous millennia. What have we gained? What have we lost?

These are open questions, and I do not pretend to have answers. Personally, I acknowledge that I benefit from many of the technological advances that we now depend on. But clearly we have lost the Eros that permeated social intercourse and individual sensibilities before a Logos mentality forsook all that. Eros is love incarnate, incorporating the physical, the spiritual and the imagination. Eros is relatedness/relationship. with others and with oneself. Logos is bottom-line thinking by economists and physicists—bloodless tit for tat, so to speak.

I am an unabashed champion of the irrational (call it Eros, why not), especially as it impinges on relationships. I am saying that love, though perhaps understandable in terms of psychology and typology, is essentially irrational. People fall in love with elephants, turtles, dogs, cats, even badgers and other humans. All that defies Logos.

Every night around midnight, it is always a choice whether to go to bed or continue searching my heart for one sentence after another.

This night I succumb to the lure of bed, but not without repeating this tune to tuck me in:

> It begins to tell round midnight, midnight.
> Supper time I'm feelin' sad,
> but it really gets bad round midnight
> Memories always start round midnight, midnight.
> Haven't got the heart to stand those memories
> When my heart is still with you
> And old midnight knows it too

When some quarrel we've had needs mending
Does it mean that our love is ending?
Darlin', I need you,
Lately I find You're out of my heart and I'm out of my mind
Let our hearts take wing round midnight, midnight
Let the angels sing for your returning
Till our love is safe and sound
When old midnight comes around.[65]

Always hard to go to bed when there's no one waiting there for me. My woman's waiting is a measure of her love; her responsive body is immeasurably a sign of her caring. I would be lost without El Jay. I dare not imagine my desperation without her.

The other night, after a delightful frolic, I said to El Jay, "Hey, I am thirty years your senior. You are at the peak of your feminine sensuality. I peaked about fifty years ago. You're okay with that?"

She pulled me closer and smiled. "You silly, I am completely happy. Experience trumps hydraulics."

Not a comment I cared to argue with. However, I am half-afraid she will wake up one morning and realize that I bore her stiff. Put it down to "negative intuition." It has no foundation in fact and suggests a shadowy fear that I am unworthy.

.

When some quarrel we've had needs mending Does it mean that our love is ending? Darlin', I need you, lately I find You're out of my heart, I'm out of my mind. Let the angels sing for your returning Till our love is safe and sound. Till old midnight comes around.

In my lonely turret, I tune in a lot to the radio, listening for a funny or incredible news item, and so on. There is so much depressing news on the radio that it is heartening to find absurd minutia like these:

1. Rats, after cockroaches, are the most hated animals on earth. It is an urban myth that in New York City there is one rat for every human; the

---

[65] Amy Winehouse, "Round Midnight," by songwriters Cootie Williams, Bernard D. Hanighen, Thelonious S. Monk; Ascap.

truth is that there are only about one-quarter as many rats as humans. So when you use the expression, "It's a rat's ass," chances are you are speaking of your own.

2. A county in Texas became concerned last year that their citizens weren't drinking enough tap water, preferring soda pop instead. So they enacted a by-law allowing them to spike their water with sugar— approximately four tablespoonfuls per eight ounces. Since doing so in November 2012, consumption of tap water has grown by eighty percent, and pop sales have plummeted. Coca Cola Inc. and Pepsico are considering legal action.

3. Gaylord Bletchley IV, Conservative backbencher in the British Parliament, rose to his feet this week to plead for Britain's citizenry to become aware that England subsidizes "Bonga-Bonga" land to the tune of two billion pounds annually. His plea was ignored, except for his term "bonga-bonga," for which he was accused of racism. Mr. Bletchley pointed to Webster's Dictionary, where bonga is defined as "a white antelope"…

****

Writing a book entails putting one sentence after another. To do this successfully, you need a decent vocabulary, a good knowledge of syntax and sentence structure, punctuation and grammar. Of course you must also know how to parse a sentence. Then you sweat blood over every word and sentence, bleed over every paragraph. You don't need to be perfect; you can always hire a professional editor to clean it up. But you need to know the basics to even begin.

Staring at the wall, I am writing , writing, writing in my head.

****

As I was struggling here to put one word after another, I heard an interview on the radio with a British novelist, Jeanette Winterson. She spoke of her recent novel *Oranges Aren't the Only Fruit*. It sounded interesting, so I immediately ordered it from my local library, and picked it up just yesterday. Well, I can tell you that the introduction is so interesting that I almost didn't bother to read the rest of the book.

But I did, and it is absolutely spellbinding. I read it non-stop for three days, ignoring everything—emails, family and friends, my own work. All was dross that was not *Oranges*. I can hardly tell you how enthralled I was and encouraged to continue with writing my own book (I mean this one) with its whimsical and oblique narrative. I saw a kindred soul in Ms. Winterson, although her story had nothing to do with my own except, perhaps, its non-linear, disjointed structure.

Make no mistake about it, *Oranges* is a masterpiece. The prose is so succinct and direct, it melts your heart. What is it about? Well, briefly, a young girl is dominated and tormented by her witchy Bible-thumping mother until at the age of fourteen she falls in love with another young girl, Melanie. Needless to say, this has to be top secret, and physically it doesn't amount to anything except touching each other's burgeoning breasts and giggling.

Given my inveterate heterosexual nature, it is not easy for me to get into the mind of any homosexual, let alone a gay adolescent girl. However, the author/narrator Jeanette makes that pretty easy, and sometimes funny, though as earnest and honest as any first young love. The point is that Jeanette has found a friend with whom she can share thoughts away from her mother's smothering clutches. It is a "coming of age" story with implications for those of any age. I wish I could write as fluently as Ms. Winterson does. I came to love Jeanette as if she were in my arms.

****

I am currently preparing for publication an extraordinary manuscript entitled *The Love Drama of C. G. Jung: As Revealed in His Life and in His Red Book*. It tracks Jung's amours through his attachment to his wife Emma, his affair with Sabina Spielrein and his life-long love relationship with Toni Wolff, showing how these conflicting loves manifested in Jung's *Red Book* and resulted in his concepts of anima, shadow and Self. This is an exciting and well-researched book about midlife, conflict, personal integrity and individuation. Do not miss it.

****

This morning, a Sunday, alone in my turret and with nothing much in the works, an inner voice prompted me to have a try at writing my obituary. Just the bare facts:

Daryl Leonard Merle Sharp (code name Daemon) was born in Regina, Saskatchewan, on Jan. 2, 1936. It was a caesarian birth; he was born a Capricorn. As a child he tended to pout, earning him the nickname of Louie the Lip," and to this day some relatives still call him Lou. His maternal grandparents had emigrated to Canada from Odessa in Ukraine.

Daryl's mother Marion was a chorus girl, a "flapper" in the "roaring twenties," his father Emery initially a brakeman on the Canadian National Railway (CNR) and later an accountant in the Royal Canadian Air Force (RCAF). Daryl had one brother, two years older, who bullied him from time to time, though with affection. Daryl's mother took Eros into the kitchen, where she held the family together. She always claimed Daryl was named after the movie mogul Darryl F. Zanuck, but she couldn't account for the difference in spelling. One of Daryl's middle names came from his uncle Len, a feckless prairies boozer; the other from his father's brother Merle, a sober accountant with the Royal Bank of Canada in Regina.

The Sharp family moved frequently from one air force base to another across Canada, spending a year or so in each province, ending up in Greenwood, Nova Scotia, where Daryl completed his high school years at Middleton Regional High School at the head of his class. He excelled at badminton, basketball, snooker, table tennis, and had a rep as a ladies man. He read only science-fiction, publishing and distributing his own fan-zine at the age of sixteen. His only ambition was to emulate Hugo Gernsbach, publisher of *Amazing Stories* and a multitude of other sci-fi magazines.

Just in time, father Emery was posted to Ottawa in 1953, It was timely, for Daryl had won a scholarship to Carleton University in Ottawa, where he spent the next four years acquiring a B.Sc. in maths and physics and a post-graduate degree in journalism while he was president of the Students' Council. This was just before Carleton moved from its constricted quarters with 750 students in an old Teachers' College building to its luxurious new campus with a current enrolment of about 40,000.

After graduation in 1957, Daryl was wooed by several conglomerates, and finally recruited by Procter & Gamble for the then-princely salary of $3,000 a year. He moved to Toronto, where he had an office and title as Director of Public Relations for Canada, He was twenty-one years old; he had a midnight-blue suit and a key to the executive washroom. He had several cameras and a buxom secretary named Gladys. His Bible was Dale Carnegie's *How To Win Friends and Influence People*. He was head of the bowling team. He was editor of the in-house magazine *Moonbeams*. He lived in a fraternity house in the downtown core and had a reputation as a dynamite dancer.

Daryl was happy. He loved his job. He photographed factory workers and wrote little articles about their lives. All was well until he fell in with some literary friends who mocked him as Organization Man and convinced him that his talents were wasted at P & G. Daryl had repressed ambitions as a writer, and so, for the first time ever, he was conflicted. He chewed on this for many months.

At last, in 1959, with savings of $1,000, Daryl chose a twin-screw steamer to France over a 1958 Thunderbird convertible. On board this slow-moving little ship with maybe 300 passengers, for two weeks Daryl produced the daily newsletter slipped under doors at 8 a.m., and won the ping pong tournament. He found no pretty ladies to romance, but he kept busy writing about his experiences.

The boat docked in Le Havre. It was a short train trip to Paris, where Daryl had a rollicking time on the Left Bank as a struggling writer until his money ran out. He then debouched to England, where he found ready employment for awhile as a substitute teacher in high schools and packing books in the prestigious Harrod's department store.

In 1960 Daryl went back to Canada and landed a job with Canadian Press (CP). This work was much too boring, and so he applied to the Berlitz School for an assignment teaching English abroad, which he was given in the heartland of Germany, Bad Kreuznach (near Mainz). This was an enlightening experience that improved his German, but he could barely survive on 400 marks ($100) a month, so he returned to Toronto, where he again secured freelance editorial work with publishers. After a few months, desperate to return to England, through a friend he secured a seat on a rhesus monkey flight out of Moncton, New Brunswick to Manchester, England.

Daryl was now twenty-three years old. Soon after he returned to London he became besotted with an elegant and intelligent young ex-pat (call her B.), whom he enticed to go to the south of France and live with him in a tent on the side of a hill in a small fishing village (Sette).[66] They then toured Europe on her scooter for several months, making love whenever and wherever. It was idyllic until B. became pregnant. They returned to London, where they married in Chelsea Old Church. For a few years they lived catch-as-catch-can in Chelsea, Putney, Devon, and finally in a seventeenth-century thatched cottage in the small hamlet of Heyshott, near Midhurst, in West Sussex, where Daryl worked on his manuscripts in a shed at the foot of the garden and compiled indexes for London publishers. All very romantic.

Daryl, obsessed with European writers like Kafka, Rilke, Kierkegaard, Nietzsche, and Dostoyevsky, applied to the new University of Sussex in Brighton for the post-graduate M.A. degree in literature and philosophy, code-named "The Modern European Mind." He was accepted and excelled, and the next year he was recommended to an exchange position at the University of Dijon in France. Daryl and B. jumped at the chance. To finance their impending cross-channel adventure, Daryl took a job as a common laborer rebuilding the Waterloo Bridge; his wage was 2 and 6 — two shillings and six pence—an hour. Not much, but it added up over a few weeks, eight hours a day plus overtime.

In Dijon Daryl planned to do a Ph.D. thesis called "In Search of the Self," drawing on the work of Soren Kierkegaard ("The Religious Self"), D.H. Lawrence ("The Vital Self"), and Jean-Jacques Rousseau ("The Natural Self"). Rousseau's papers were archived in the University of Dijon, and Daryl's French was adequate to the task. In exchange, Daryl

---

[66] This love affair has been exhaustively recorded in Sharp's book, *Live Your Nonsense.*

would teach a few weekly classes in English, and once a month would partake of the 6-course all-male dinner with wines from the Route du Grand Cru. B. did not relish being left out, but that was the protocol.

It was not an easy year in Dijon. For the first month they lived in a youth hostel with their two kids, until a humble apartment was found for them in a building where thirty residents shared one outdoor toilet.

Back in England in 1966, Daryl's painstaking thesis was rejected as "expository but not original." This put an end to his shadowy aspirations for an academic career, but proved to be salutary in retrospect.

In 1967 their third child was born, Tanya, named after Henry Miller's lover in *The Tropic of Cancer.*

In 1969, the Sharp family decided to return to Canada and live in B.'s inherited house in Burlington, Ontario. This move was accomplished with no small labors, but being back in Canada was a happy time for awhile. Daryl found work with some publishers in Toronto, founded the seminal Playrights Co-Op and commuted back and forth. However, all was not well on the home front. Daryl could not abide mowing grass for six hours a week, and he was not cut out to be "the (handy) man around the house." B. too was not happy. They both turned to others for solace.

The climax came when Daryl was dislodging a beehive in the eaves and was stung by a bee. He went into anaphylactic shock and spent two days in the hospital. He underwent allergy treatments for a year, but it turned out he was only allergic to B. The symbolism did not escape him.

In 1973, with Daryl's relationship with B. in tatters, he flew back to England to go into Jungian analysis. Much happened in between, but in 1978 Daryl graduated from the Jung Institute in Zurich with a Diploma in Jungian psychology, and then returned to Toronto and the three children he loved and had missed. He found a new mate, Vicki, with whom he fathered Jessy Kate (code name JK), later to become an astrophysicist working for NASA.

Daryl Sharp was no idiot savant, though some claim he was an idiot, if not wise, to found a publishing house in 1980 catering exclusively to a niche Jungian market. However, over time this modest enterprise (never more than two people) earned him almost a million dollars, most of which he gave to his kids to buy their houses or to shelters for abused women.

Sharp (or "Razr," as he was sometimes known) led a rather shadowy life alongside his meagre practice as a Jungian analyst. He smoked (rolling his own) and drank Scotch, both to excess. He was a notorious womanizer in his youth, flirting outrageously with other men's wives. This did not endear him to his male peers, but women adored his wit and playfulness, to the extent that many a hitherto chaste lass was known to come awry in his presence.

He leaves behind his two sons, Dave and Ben, two daughters, Tanya Clair and Jessy Kate, and his many friends.

And above his ashes in the Rose Garden of Mount Pleasant Cemetery in Toronto, a bronze plaque reads, at his request:

"He was kind and generous; he loved women."

That was hard to write, but better me than a rookie on the Canadian Press obit desk. They'll cut it anyway.

****

Seniors beware! About twenty years ago, a lone maniac poisoned a single bottle of Tylenol. Since then, pharmaceutical products have been sealed so tight with safety caps that it takes a screwdriver or pliers to get into your meds. Even my weekly "medication organizer," delivered every Friday evening, needs scissors to release the pills. This pharma overreaction must also add to the cost of products.

I could extend this observation to virtually everything we buy nowadays. On top of the excessive packaging, there are extensive instructions on how to open that are challenging if not impossible to follow, and seldom work as claimed. Resealable? Dontcha believe it; just another marketing ploy, like those solar panelists who try to convince us to save 80% on electricity when we don't even have a west- or south-facing roof.

It is very discouraging, this capitalist society. Wherever you turn, someone's out to make a buck. Well, I should not gainsay it absolutely, for I make my living that way too, Well, we all have to eat. What I object to is extortion and advertising or marketing swindles. And books are not hard to get into.

****

When I was eighteen, I dared to ask my father how he won "fair lady," i.e., my mother, for she was certainly a beauty in her chorus-girl days and always in my eyes.

My dad nursed his beer and replied thoughtfully, "Every day, I told her I loved her."

And so to this very day I say the same to my current sweetheart. It doesn't always stop Thursday from colliding with Friday, but it makes me feel happy.

> Desire is so fragile
> it flies or dies on a whim,
> Wants or doesn't her or him.
> What is one to do
> but go with the flow.
> This is hard to learn.
> It makes me squirm
> Just to think of it.

****

I think I will have to stop watching TV dramas. The problem is that I identify so much with various characters that I lose my own footing. Of course I should know better, but look to yourself and think of how we are all blind-sided by our shadow.

For instance, I may drink a lot, mostly in order to stay awake and write about what passes through my mind—much of it nonsense or whimsical, granted, but essentially my truth. So sue me for being authentic, throw the first stone.

****

I do so enjoy falling in love, that first flush of passionate infatuation when you can't keep your hands off each other and spend half your time together in bed or playing cribbage. Every kiss, every touch, is almost too much. It is a transcendent experience entirely inspiriting and sweeps you away. You do everything you can think of to please the other. You forget appointments, push work aside and focus on play. Romance and relationship are paramount. Heart leaps, head spins. You cook for each other and exchange billets doux. She lets you sleep in while she makes you breakfast, or vice versa. There is no rhyme or logic to your feelings. You gift her pearls and she responds by unloading your dishwasher. You are comfortable with each other, and you feel companionable. You are both afloat on the wings of Eros, and Beelzebub take the hindmost.

It is altogether an ecstatic experience to be in love.

That first stage of love, the "honeymoon phase," may last a few days or weeks, months, even years. However long, it is an other-worldly, magical time of transcendence, as long as Thursday does not collide with Friday.

In my personal lexicon of love, Thursday equates with *anima,* man's inner woman, and *animus/*Friday with woman's inner man. These terms have gained considerable currency since Jung coined them more than a hundred years ago, but their significance in relationships is still little understood. I think they should be taught in high school so teenagers would have an idea of what they are in for psychologically in their current and future love relationships.

The early and medieval female saints, and even as recently as Joan of Arc (executed in 1431), ascribed their ecstasy to the requited love for Jesus.

I do not find this an adequate explanation for their visions and dreams. Indeed, Marie-Louise von Franz sees their love of Christ as projections of the animus.[67]

Okay, just anther fantasy. But what am I to do here at 2 a.m. listening to jazz make me cooler, and awaiting a lovely lady to drag me off to bed? At the same time, I am glad to be on my own. Welcome to the opposites, Jung 201. I hold the tension and await the symbolic manifestation of the transcendent function, which I hope I will be sentient enough to recognize. I am a tired old hack, after all, if not actually an elderly badger.

Well, I lived so long in the clutches of Logos that no wonder Eros

---

[67] See *The Passion of Perpetua: A Psychological Interpretation of Her Visions,* pp. 31ff..

inevitably overwhelmed me. In case you've forgotten, it is called *enantiodromia* (the process whereby opposites switch places over time).

> Willow weep for me, willow weep for me,
> Bend your branches green along the stream that runs to sea,
> Listen to my plea, listen willow weep for me,
> Gone my lover's dream, lovely summer dream,
> Gone and left me here to weep my tears into the stream,
> Sad as I can be - Hear me willow and weep for me.
>
> Whisper to the wind to say that love has sinned
> To leave my heart aching and making this moan,
> Murmur to the night to hide her starry light,
> So none will find me sighing and crying all alone,
> Weeping willow tree, weep in sympathy,
> Bend your branches down along the ground and cover me,
> When the shadows fall, bend oh willow and weep for me.
>
> To leave my heart aching and making this moan,
> So none will find me sighing and crying all alone,
> Weeping willow tree, weep in sympathy,
> Bend your branches down along the ground and cover me,
> When the shadows fall, bend oh willow,
> Bend oh willow and weep for me.[68]

****

No matter how you cut it, doing the laundry is a pain in the arse.

For many years I toted an old broken plastic brown basket down the stairs from the second floor to the basement washing machine and dryer. Then my friend Rebecca gifted me a string bag which I could fill and drop over the balcony to the ground floor, and then throw it down the basement stairs, a few steps away from the washer. A lot better than the plastic basket, but I still find the process tiring.

I recently consulted a contractor about installing a small apartment-sized washer and dryer on my second floor. Alas, we could not find a

---

[68] Jerome Kern, Otto Harbach, Ann Ronell; Ascap.

place it would work without destroying walls and ceilings for the plumbing, altogether an unacceptable disruption.

So doing the laundry, no matter how you cut it, is still a pain in the arse, only not as much as it used to be without the string bag. Bless Rebecca for that and much more. But to look at it symbolically, doing the laundry does put you in touch with your shadow, your dirt. I am cheered by that thought.

Changing the subject, I have a fantasy of this year escaping the familial responsibilities that go with the Christmas-New Year season. As patriarch, I can do what I want, and no one would chide me. So what do I want?

Well, today I browsed through a brochure touting a yoga retreat on Paradise Island in Nassau, Bahamas. Well, I've been there several times, not for the yoga, which I actually didn't enjoy, but for the loving I experienced at the time with my exotic sweetheart on the beach and in her tent. To be fair, it was a very healthy two weeks, with vegetarian meals twice a day, meditation sessions, no alcohol or tobacco, and a regimen that included being up at 6 a.m., in bed by 10, and a glorious beach. It is certainly a good place for a retreat from work and the hustle and bustle of the Big City, even if you don't like yoga.

Now, even with a loving companion, it's likely that I wouldn't have much fun there, so I am shelving that idea. I have said it before, but travelling is quite boring without a lover, and with one you can enjoy going anywhere.

An attractive alternative for me is a sojourn on Costa Rica at La Choza, burgeoning think tank established by my daughter JK. It is thirty acres of relatively untamed jungle, nature, peace and quiet.[69] Her international cohort, friends interested in communal living, is gathering there for the coming holiday season. I am invited, and I do like the idea of joining them, but I'm not sure I am up to the travel.

****

Thanks to the flip side of my positive mother complex, I live on the edge,

---

[69] See chozadelmundo.com.

always anticipating the wrath of a woman for something I've said, done, or not. This is clearly a defense against disappointment, but I am usually surprised by the simple joy of being accepted by an other, which happens more often than not. Well, I live in a world of opposites, where whatever I think or do has its compensating counterpart (call it shadow, why not?)

****

Rest my case, your Honor. Good night.

Watch for Book Three of the **Badger Trilogy.**

Drawing by Leigh Hobbs in
Mr. Badger and the Magic Mirror.

BIBLIOGRAPHY
(with recommended reading)

Carotenuto, Aldo. *Eros and Pathos: Shades of Love and Suffering.* Toronto: Inner City Books, 1989.

Cohen, Leonard. *Book of Longing.* Toronto: McClelland & Stewart Ltd., 2006.

Daumal, René. *Mount Analogue: An Authentic Narrative.* Trans. and Intro. Robert Shattuck. London, UK: Vincent Stuart Publishers Ltd., 1959.

De Vries, Ad. *Dictionary of Symbols and Imagery.* Amsterdam: North-Holland Publishing Company, 1976.

Edinger, Edward F. *Anatomy of the Psyche: Alchemical Symbolism in Psychotherapy.* La Salle, IL: Open Court, 1985.

_____. *The Creation of Consciousness: Jung's Myth for Modern Man.* Toronto: Inner City Books, 1984.

_____. "M. Esther Harding, 1888-1971." In *Spring 1972.* Zurich: Spring Publications, 1972.

_____. *The Mysterium Lectures: A Journey Through Jung's* Mysterium Coniunctionis. Toronto: Inner City Books, 1995.

_____. *The Mystery of the Coniunctio: Alchemical Image of Individuation.* Toronto: Inner City Books, 1994.

_____. *Transformation of the God-Image: An Elucidation of Jung's* Answer to Job. Toronto: Inner City Books, 1992.

_____. *Science of the Soul: A Jungian Perspective.* Toronto: Inner City Books, 2002.

Elder, George R., and Cordic, Dianne D., eds. *An American Jungian: In Honor of Edward F. Edinger.* Toronto: Inner City Books, 2009.

Eliot, T. S. *Four Quartets.* London, UK: Faber and Faber Limited, 1959.

Ellenberger, Henri, *The Discovery of the Unconscious: The History and Evolution of Dynamic Psychiatry.* New York: Basic Books, 1970.

Emerson, Ralph Waldo. *Essays: First and Second Series.* Intr. Douglas Crase. New York: Penguin Books (Library of America), 2010.

_____. *Selected Journals, 1841-1877.* New York: Penguin Books (Library of America), 2010.

Epicurus and the Epicurean Tradition. Ed. Jeffrey Fish and Kirk R. Sanders. Cambridge, UK: Cambridge University Press, 2012.

Frey-Rohn, Liliane. *From Freud to Jung: A Comparative Study of the Psychology of the Unconscious.* Boston: Shambhala Publications, 1974.

Frost, Robert. "Stopping by Woods on a Snowy Evening." In "The Poetry of Robert Frost," Ed. Edward Connery Lathem, from *The Random House Book of Poetry for Children.* New York: Random House, 1983.

Grimm Brothers. *The Complete Grimm's Fairy Tales.* New York: Pantheon Books, 1944.

Greenblatt, Stephen. *The Swerve: How the World Became Modern.* New York: W.W. Norton & Company, 2011.

Hall, James A., and Sharp, Daryl, eds. *Marie-Louise von Franz: The Classic Jungian and the Classic Jungian Tradition.* Toronto: Inner City Books, 2008.

Hannah, Barbara. *Jung: His Life and Work (A Biographical Memoir).* New York: Capricorn Books, G.P. Putnam's Sons, 1976.

Hobbs, Leigh. *Mr. Badger and the Magic Mirror.* Crows Nest, Australia: Allen & Unwin, 2011.

Hollis, James. *The Middle Passage: From Misery to Meaning in Midlife.* Toronto: Inner City Books, 1993.

_____. *The Eden Project: In Search of the Magical Other.* Toronto: Inner City Books, 1998.

_____. *Under Saturn's Shadow: The Wounding and Healing of Men.* Toronto: Inner City Books, 1994.

Jacoby, Mario. *The Analytic Encounter: Transference and Human Relationship.* Toronto: Inner City Books, 1984.

_____. *Longing for Paradise: Psychological Perspectives on an Archetype.* Toronto: Inner City Books, 2006.

Jaffe, Lawrence. *Liberating the Heart: Preparing for the New Religion.* Toronto: Inner City Books, 1990.

Jung, C. G. *C. G. Jung Letters.* (Bollingen Series XCV). 2 vols. Ed. G. Adler and A. Jaffé. Princeton: Princeton University Press, 1973.

_____. *The Collected Works of C. G. Jung* (Bollingen Series XX). 20 vols. Trans. R. F. C. Hull. Ed. H. Read, M. Fordham, G. Adler, Wm. McGuire. Princeton: Princeton University Press, 1953-1979.

_____. *Memories, Dreams, Reflections.* Ed. Aniela Jaffé. New York: Pantheon Books, 1961.

_____. *The Psychology of Kundalini Yoga: Notes of the Seminar Given in 1932 by C.G. Jung* (Bollingen Series XCIX). Ed. Sonu Shamdasani. Princeton: Princeton University Press, 1996.

_____. *Visions: Notes of the Seminar Given in 1930-1934* (Bollingen Series XCIX). 2 vols. Ed. Claire Douglas. Princeton: Princeton Univ. Press, 1997.

Jung, Carl G., and von Franz, Marie-Louise, eds. *Man and His Symbols.* London, UK: Aldus Books, 1964.

Kafka, Franz. [D1] *The Diaries of Franz Kafka, 1910-1913.* Trans. Joseph Kresh. Ed. Max Brod. London: Secker & Warburg, 1948.

_____. [D2] *The Diaries of Franz Kafka, 1914-1923.* Trans. Martin Greenberg. Ed. Max Brod. London: Secker & Warburg, 1949.

_____. *The Great Wall of China and Other Pieces.* Trans. Willa and Edwin Muir. London: Secker & Warburg, 1946.

Kaufmann, Walter, ed. and trans. *The Portable Nietzsche.* New York: Viking Press, 1954.

Kierkegaard, Søren. *The Journals of Kierkegaard: 1834-1854.* Ed. and trans. Alexander Dru. Oxford, UK: Oxford University Press, 1958.

Lucretius, Titus: *On the Nature of Things,* trans. H.A.J. Munro. In *Lucretius; Epictetus; M. Aurelius.* Chicago: William Benton, 1952.

Luton, Frith. *Bees, Honey and the Hive: Circumambulating the Centre (A Jungian Exploration of the Symbolism and Psychology).* Toronto: Inner City Books, 2011.

Malcolm, Janet. *Psychoanalysis: The Impossible Profession.* New York: Alfred A. Knopf, 1981.

McGuire, William, ed. *The Freud/Jung Letters* (Bollingen Series XCIV). Trans. Ralph Manheim and R. F. C. Hull. Princeton: Princeton University Press, 1974.

McGuire, William, and Hull, R. F. C., eds. *C. G. Jung Speaking: Interviews and Encounters* (Bollingen Series XCVII). Princeton: Princeton University Press, 1977.

Meredith, Margaret Eileen. *The Secret Garden: Temenos for Individuation.* Toronto: Inner City Books, 2005.

Miller, Henry. *The Wisdom of the Heart.* New York: New Directions, 1950.

Monick, Eugene. *Phallos: Sacred Image of the Masculine.* Toronto: Inner City Books, 1987.

Nietzsche, Friedrich, *The Portable Nietzsche.* Trans. with Intro., WalterKaufmann. New York: Viking Press, 1954.

Perera, Sylvia Brinton. *Descent to the Goddess: A Way of Initiation for Women.* Toronto: Inner City Books, 1981.

_____. *The Scapegoat Complex: Toward a Mythology of Shadow and Guilt.* Toronto: Inner City Books, 1986.

Plato. *The Dialogues of Plato.* New York: Random House, 1965.

Qualls-Corbett, Nancy. *The Sacred Prostitute: Eternal Aspect of the Feminine.* Toronto: Inner City Books, 1988.

Rank, Otto. *The Trauma of Birth.* New York: Brunner, 1952.

Rilke, Rainer Maria. *Letters on Cezanne.* New York: Fromm International, 1985.

_____.*The Notebook of Malte Laurids Brigge.* Trans. John Linton. London, UK: The Hogarth Press, 1959.

_____. *Rilke on Love and Other Difficulties.* Ed. John Mood. New York, Norton, 1975.

_____. *Rainer Maria Rilke, Sonnets to Orpheus.* Trans. Willis Barnstone. Boston, MA: Shambhala, 2004.

Seuss, Dr. *You're only Old Once: A Book for Obsolete Children.* New York: Random House, 1986.

Sharp, Daryl. *The Brillig Trilogy.* See below: *Chicken Little; Who Am I, Really?;* and *Living Jung.*

_____. *Chicken Little: The Inside Story (a Jungian romance).* Toronto: Inner City Books, 1993.

_____. *C. G. Jung Lexicon: A Primer of Terms and Concepts.* Toronto: Inner City Books, 1991.

_____. *Dear Gladys: The Survival Papers, Book 2.* Toronto: Inner City Books, 1989.

_____. *Digesting Jung: Food for the Journey.* Toronto: Inner City Books, 2001.

_____. *The Eros Trilogy.* See *Live Your Nonsense; Trampled to Death by Gees;,* and *Hijacked by Eros.*

_____. *Eyes Wide Open: Late Thoughts (a Jungian romance).* Toronto: Inner City Books, 2007.

_____. *Getting To Know You: The Inside Out of Relationship.* Toronto: Inner City Books, 1992.

_____. *Jung Uncorked: Rare Vintages from the Cellar of Analytical Psychology.* 4 vols. Toronto: Inner City Books, 2008-9.

_____. *Jungian Psychology Unplugged: My Life as an Elephant.* Toronto, Inner City Books, 1998.

_____. *Live Your Nonsense: Halfway to Dawn with Eros (A Jungian Perspective on Individuation).* Toronto: Inner City Books, 2010.

_____. *Living Jung: The Good and the Better.* Toronto: Inner City Books, 1966.

_____. *Miles To Go Before I Sleep: Growing Up Puer (another Jungian romance).* Toronto: Inner City Books, 2013.

_____. *Not the Big Sleep: On Having Fun, Seriously (a Jungian romance).* Toronto: Inner City Books, 2005.

_____. *On Staying Awake: Getting Older and Bolder (another Jungian romance).* Toronto: Inner City Books, 2006.

_____. *Personality Types: Jung's Model of Typology.* Toronto: Inner City Books, 1987.

_____. *The Secret Raven: Conflict and Transformation in the Life of Franz Kafka.* Toronto: Inner City Books, 1980.

_____. *The SleepNot Trilogy.* See *Not the Big Sleep; On Staying Awake; and Eyes Wide Open.*

_____. *The Survival Papers: Anatomy of a Midlife Crisis.* Toronto: Inner City Books, 1988.

_____. *Trampled to Death by Geese: More Eros, and a Lot More Nonsense (A Jungian analyst's whimsical perspective on the Inner Life).* Toronto: Inner City Books, 2011.

_____. *Who Am I, Really? Personality, Soul and Individuation.* Toronto: Inner City Books, 1995.

Sparks, J. Gary. *At the Heart of Matter: Synchronicity and Jung's Spiritual Testament.* Toronto: Inner City Books, 2007.

_____. *In the Valley of Diamonds: Adventures in* Number and Time *with Marie-Louise von Franz.* Toronto: Inner City Books, 2009.

Stein, Gertrude. *Geography and Plays.* New York: Random House, 1922.

Stevens, Anthony. *Archetype Revisited: An Updated Natural History of the Self.* Toronto: Inner City Books, 2003.

_____. *The Talking Cure: Psychotherapy, Past, Present and Future.* 3 vols. Toronto: Inner City Books, 2013.

Storr, Anthony. *Solitude.* London, UK: HarperCollins Publishers, 1997.

Von Franz, Marie-Louise. *The Passion of Perpetua: A Psychological Interpretation of Her Visions.* Toronto: Inn City Books, 2004.

_____. *The Problem of the Puer Aeternus.* Toronto: Inner City Books, 2000.

Winterson, Jeanette. *Oranges Are Not the Only Fruit.* London, UK: Vintage Books, 2011.

_____. *Why Be Happy When You Could Be Normal?* Toronto: Alfred A. Knopf Canada, 2011.

Yeoman, Ann. *Now Or Neverland: A Psychological Perspective on a Cultural Icon.* Toronto: Inner City Books, 1998.

Index

"whore's cellar," 60
Whyte, William: *Organization Man,* 72
Wilkes, Dr. C.T., 24
"Willow weep for me," 94
Winehouse, Amy, 42, 85n
"Winships, Breaking Up of the," 70
Winterson, Jeanette: *Oranges Aren't the Only Fruit,* 86
women, *See also anima;animus;* feminine mystique; feminism/feminists
Wolff, Toni, 87
Woolf, Virginia, 46
writing, writing complex, 6, 73-76, 80-81, 87-88

Wylie, Philip: *Generation of Vipers,* 72

Yeoman, Ann: *Now or Neverland,* 72n
yoga, 95
yoke(d), 54-56
yoni, 38, 77
"You Made Me Love You," 50
"You're a Sweetheart," 19
"You've Got a Friend," 21-22

Zurich, 26, 43. *See also* Sharp, Daryl

Also in this Series by Daryl Sharp

Please see next page for discounts and postage/handling.

THE SECRET RAVEN: Conflict and Transformation in the Life of Franz Kafka
ISBN 978-0-919123-00-7. (1980) 128 pp. $25

PERSONALITY TYPES: Jung's Model of Typology
ISBN 978-0-919123-30-9. (1987) 128 pp. $25. *(Free PDF on website.)*

THE SURVIVAL PAPERS: Anatomy of a Midlife Crisis
ISBN 978-0-919123-34-2. (1988) 160 pp. $25

DEAR GLADYS: The Survival Papers, Book 2
ISBN 978-0-919123-36-6. (1989) 144 pp. $25

JUNG LEXICON: A Primer of Terms and Concepts
ISBN 978-0-919123-48-9. (1991) 160 pp. $25. *(Free PDF on website.)*

GETTING TO KNOW YOU: The Inside Out of Relationship
ISBN 978-0-919123-56-4. (1992) 128 pp. $25

THE BRILLIG TRILOGY:

    1. CHICKEN LITTLE: The Inside Story *(A Jungian romance)*
    ISBN 978-0-919123-62-5. (1993) 128 pp. $25. *(Free PDF on website.)*

    2. WHO AM I, REALLY? Personality, Soul and Individuation
    ISBN 978-0-919123-68-7. (1995) 144 pp. $25

    3. LIVING JUNG: The Good and the Better
    ISBN 978-0-919123-73-1. (1996) 128 pp. $25

JUNGIAN PSYCHOLOGY UNPLUGGED: My Life as an Elephant
ISBN 978-0-919123-81-6. (1998) 160 pp. $25

DIGESTING JUNG: Food for the Journey
ISBN 978-0-919123-96-0. (2001) 128 pp. $25. *(Free PDF on website.)*

JUNG UNCORKED: Rare Vintages from the Cellar of Analytical
Psychology. 4 vols. 128 pp. each. $25 each

THE SLEEPNOT TRILOGY:

    1. NOT THE BIG SLEEP: On having fun, seriously *(A Jungian romance)*
    ISBN 978-0-894574-13-6. (2005) 128 pp. $25. *(Free PDF on website.)*

    2. ON STAYING AWAKE: Getting Older and Bolder *(Another Jungian romance)*
    ISBN 978-0-894574-16-7. (2006) 144 pp. $25

    3. EYES WIDE OPEN: Late Thoughts *(Another Jungian romance)*
    ISBN 978-0-894574-18-1.. (2007) 160 pp. $25

Studies in Jungian Psychology
by Jungian Analysts   *Quality Paperbacks*

Prices and payment in $US (except in Canada, and Credit Card orders, $Cdn)

Jung Uncorked: Rare Vintages from the Cellar of Analytical Psychology, 4. vols.
Daryl Sharp (Toronto) ISBN 978-1-894574-21-1/22-8/24-2/27-3. 128 pp. each, $25 each

Jung and Yoga: The Psyche-Body Connection
Judith Harris (London, Ontario) ISBN 978-0-919123-95-3. 160 pp. $25

The Love Drama of C. G. Jung: As Revealed in His Life and in his *Red Book*.
Maria Helena Mandacarú Guerra (Sao Paulo) 978-1-894574-42-6. 128 pp. $25

Conscious Femininity: Interviews with Marion Woodman
Introduction by Marion Woodman (Toronto) ISBN 978-0-919123-59-5. 160 pp. $25

The Sacred Psyche: A Psychological Approach to the Psalms
Edward F. Edinger (Los Angeles) ISBN 978-1-894574-09-9. 160 pp. $25

Eros and Pathos: Shades of Love and Suffering
Aldo Carotenuto (Rome) ISBN 978- 0-919123-39-7. 144 pp. $25

Descent to the Goddess: A Way of Initiation for Women
Sylvia Brinton Perera (New York) ISBN 978-0-919123-05-2. 112 pp. $25

Addiction to Perfection: The Still Unravished Bride
Marion Woodman (Toronto) ISBNj 978-0-919123-11-3. Illustrated. 208 pp. $30/$35hc

The Illness That We Are: A Jungian Critique of Christianity
John P. Dourley (Ottawa) ISBN 978-0-919123-16-8. 128 pp. $25

Jungian Dream Interpretation: A Handbook of Theory and Practice
James A. Hall, M.D. (Dallas) ISBN 978-0-919123-12-0. 128 pp. $25

Phallos: Sacred Image of the Masculine
Eugene Monick (Scranton) ISBN 978-0-919123-26-7. 30 illustrations. 144 pp. $25

The Sacred Prostitute: Eternal Aspect of the Feminine
Nancy Qualls-Corbett (Birmingham) ISBN 978-0-919123-31-1. Illustrated. 176 pp. $30

The Pregnant Virgin: A Process of Psychological Development
Marion Woodman (Toronto) ISBN 978-0-919123-20-5. Illustrated. 208 pp. $30pb/$35hc

Discounts: any 3-5 books, 10%; 6-9 books, 20%; 10-19, 25%; 20 or more, 40% .

Add Postage/Handling: 1-2 books, $6 surface ($10 air); 3-4 books, $8 surface

($12 air); 5-9 books, $15 surface ($20 air); 10 or more, $15 surface ($30 air).

FREE SHIPPING via Shopping Cart on website: www.innercitybooks.net

Credit cards accepted. Toll-free Canada and U.S.: Tel. 1-888-927-0355.

INNER CITY BOOKS, Box 1271, Station Q, Toronto, ON M4T 2P4, Canada
Tel. (416) 927-0355 / sales@innercitybooks.net/ www.innercitybooks.net